Allgemeine Ausgabe

FOCUS ON SUCCESS

The new edition

Workbook

CONTENTS

Refresher Course

Main Course

A Refresher Course
Free-time activities

1 FREE-TIME ACTIVITIES

›› SB page 6, exercise 1

Read the speech bubbles and name the speaker's free time activity.

1. *Well, it can be a bit boring but when you do catch something, wow!* ____________
2. *I don't have a horse of my own. I have to borrow one.* ____________
3. *Second-hand stuff is really cheap and we have a good free library in town, too.* ____________
4. *I never bet money. No way. I play online for fun, but I play to win, of course.* ____________
5. *Fridays and Saturdays I meet some mates and we dance the night away.* ____________
6. *I don't just listen to music. I'm more creative. I generally write my own.* ____________

2 PREPOSITIONS

›› SB page 7, text

Complete the text with words and phrases from the box. Use each word/phrase once only.

about | against | around | at | for | in | in front of | off | out | out of | round | with

Many people think that young people today only spend their free time sitting ________ (1) the television. But do they really know what they are talking ________ (2)? Chilling ________ (3) and hanging ________ (4) with friends are the favourite free-time activities, according to a new survey published today. Girls like looking ________ (5) shops more than boys; they are more likely to be playing ________ (6) other players online. Many young people do sport and play ________ (7) teams; for them it is difficult to go clubbing ________ (8) the weekend, otherwise they might find themselves ________ (9) the team. Some young people also do something worthwhile, like working ________ (10) a charity. Working ________ (11) homeless people may not be everybody's idea of fun, but they obviously get a lot ________ (12) it.

3 SUBJECT AND OBJECT PRONOUNS

›› SB page 8, exercise 5

Fill in the missing pronouns.

1 Sorry. Can ________ (1) say that again? ________ (2) didn't understand ________ (3).

2 Do ________ (1) know Tom Webb? ________ (2) met ________ (3) yesterday. ________ (4)'s a champion dancer.

3 Don't give bread to the ducks. ________ (1) says on that notice that ________ (2)'s bad for ________ (3).

4 Where are Janna and Josh? ________ (1) told ________ (2) not to be late because ________ (3) must pick up our tickets by 8 o'clock or we lose ________ (4).

5 Franzi's parents are too tolerant. ________ (1)'s clear to ________ (2) that ________ (3) have a big problem with ________ (4).

6 Sarah is worried about her son. ________ (1) told ________ (2) to work harder or ________ (3) will have to take his exams again.

4 SIMPLE PRESENT

›› SB page 9, exercise 6

Use the elements to make complete sentences. Add any missing words.

1 Dana / do / voluntary work / three evenings / week

____

2 Ravi / be / football club / and / play / first team

____

3 Ravi and Jack / enjoy / clubbing but / not go / very often

____

4 how often / Lucy + go / work / each week / ?

____

5 Sal and Sam / not play / violent games /. They / prefer / test / their skill

____

6 you + have / a lot of free time / or / you + work / ?

____

5 PRESENT PROGRESSIVE

›› SB page 10, exercise 7

Use an expression from box A and a verb from box B to say what the people and animals are doing.

A ~~at the kiosk~~ | from a diving board | in blue boxer shorts | near some steps | on a bistro table | on a mobile phone | on a red blanket | a sunlounger (*Sonnenliege*) | out of the pool | under a tree

B ~~buy~~ | climb | dive | have (a picnic) | have (a shower) | jump | read | stand | sunbathe | talk

A man is buying an ice cream at the kiosk.

____

____

____

____

____

____

____

6 SIMPLE PRESENT OR PRESENT PROGRESSIVE?

›› SB pages 9–11

Cross out the incorrect form.

1 I am going / go to the fitness centre on Saturdays.

2 Alan is often reading / often reads two books a week.

3 Elle can't come to the phone now. She has / is having a shower.

4 We always do / are always doing [1] our homework as soon as we are getting / get [2] home.

5 Are you sometimes eating / Do you sometimes eat Indian food?

6 I am not liking / don't like our new neighbours much.

7 Do you plan / Are you planning a LAN party at the moment?

8 How much coffee are you drinking / do you drink a day?

9 Look! The sun comes / is coming out.

10 Sam prefers / is preferring games that test his skill.

7 SIMPLE PRESENT OR PRESENT PROGRESSIVE?

›› SB pages 9–11

Complete the sentences with the correct form of the verb in brackets.

1 Dana ____________________[1] (spend) most of her free time working with the Red Cross. This week she ____________________[2] (work) with homeless people. Her brother ____________________[3] (not/think) she ____________________[4] (enjoy) life.

2 Lucy ____________________[1] (work) three evenings a week, but this evening she ____________________[2] (do) her homework. She always ____________________[3] (enjoy) going shopping with her friends.

3 Ravi usually ____________________[1] (have) matches at the weekend. When he ____________________[2] (not/play) football he ____________________[3] (hang) around with his friends.

8 WORDFIELD: FREE-TIME ACTIVITIES

›› SB pages 6–7

Make a mindmap like the one below. Add as many different free-time activities as you can. Use your exercise book if necessary.

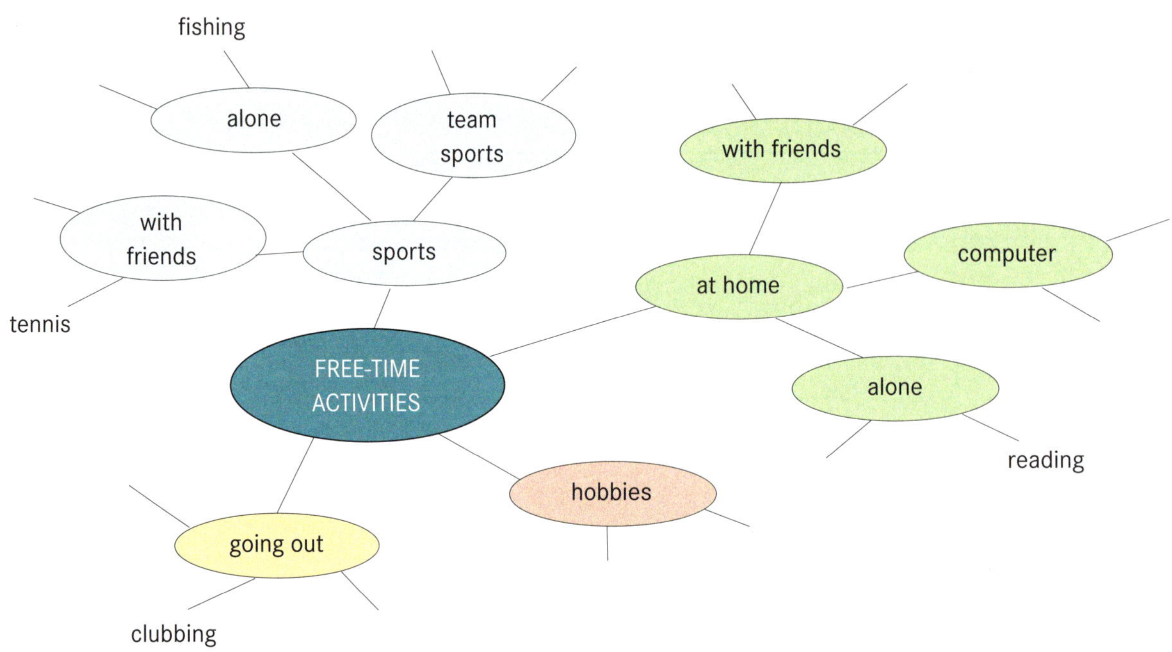

B Refresher Course
Girls fight for their rights

1 QUESTIONS AND ANSWERS

›› SB page 12, text

Match the questions 1–8 with the answers a–h.

1 How did Ashley's male teammates react at first?	f	a	Although the boy was big and strong, he was slow.
2 How do we know that Ashley's fans see her as a real fighter?		b	She means that her male opponents should fight her exactly as they would fight a boy.
3 There are not enough girls to make up an all-girl team. What's the solution?		c	In that case, girls have to join boys' teams.
4 What do you understand by "Title IX"?		d	It's overcoming chauvinistic stereotyping.
5 What does Ashley mean by "equal in every way"?		e	She had to wrestle a big boy from her school's most dangerous rival.
6 What is a girl's biggest problem about doing mixed sport?		f	Some just stared at her; others made nasty jokes.
7 What was Ashley Moore's "awesome challenge"?		g	They compare her to Xena, a fictional warrior princess.
8 Why did Ashley's opponent lose the match?		h	Title IX is a federal law against sex discrimination in US public schools.

2 WORD SEARCH

›› SB page 12, text

Underline ten English words about sport that are used in the text. They are not necessarily in the same order.

3 THE SIMPLE PAST

›› SB page 14, exercise 3

Complete the sentences with the simple past form of the underlined verb. Be careful with irregular forms.

1 We normally train on Thursdays, but last week we __________ on Wednesday.

2 Pete doesn't often win, but he __________ his fight yesterday evening.

3 **A** Did you come to training by bike? **B** No, I __________ by bus.

4 **A** Did you wear your new football boots for the match? **B** No, I __________ my old ones.

5 **A** Did you buy that football shirt at Intersport? **B** No, I __________ it online. It was cheaper.

6 **A** Did the trainer choose you for the first team? **B** Yes, but he __________ me to play in goal.

7 **A** Did Ashley take part in the tournament last weekend? **B** Yes, she did. She __________ part on both days.

8 **A** What time did you arrive here? **B** I __________ at about two o'clock, I think.

4 NEGATIVES IN THE SIMPLE PAST

›› SB page 14, exercise 3

Look at the drawings and complete the sentence. Choose a verb from the box.

buy | go | have | meet | play | score | take | watch

1 
I *didn't watch TV* last night. I ______________________.

2 
We ______________________ clubbing on Saturday.
We ______________________ to the movies.

3 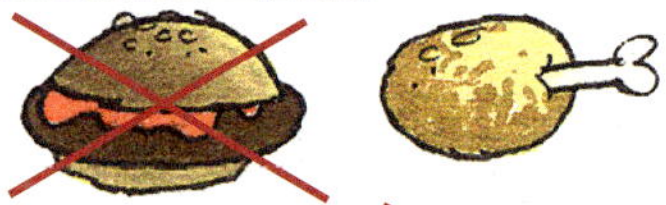
Jane ______________________.
______________________.

4 
They ______________________.
______________________.

5 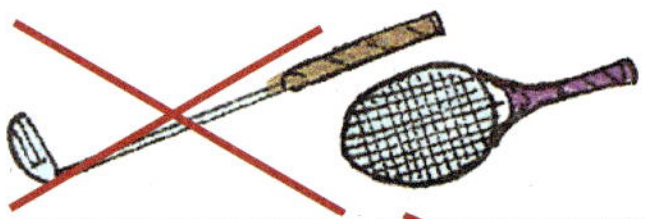
We ______________________ yesterday.
______________________.

6 

Alan ______________________,
but Revi ______________________.

7 

Tom ______________________ in town.
______________________.

8 
I ______________________ a laptop.
______________________ a desktop computer.

5 ASKING QUESTIONS ABOUT THE PAST

›› SB page 14, exercise 3

Ask questions about the highlighted part of the sentences.

1 Josh and Janna went bowling last weekend.
When *did Josh and Janna go bowling* ______________________?

2 Unfortunately, they missed their booking because of bad traffic delays.
Why ______________________?

3 In the end, they waited for over two hours for a free lane (*Bahn*).
How long ______________________?

4 They finally started their first game at 9 pm.
When ______________________ their first game?

5 However, they became angry because their lane did not work properly.
Why ______________________?

6 Josh complained to the manager about the faulty lane.
Who ______________________ the faulty lane?

7 But the problem with this was that they had to wait a long time again.
What ______________________?

8 Poor Josh and Janna finally arrived home at 2 o'clock in the morning.
When ______________________?

C

Refresher Course

You are what you eat

1 IN A RESTAURANT

›› SB page 16, text

Link the waiter's questions 1–8 to the diner's answers a–h.

1 How would you like your steak?	c	a I'll have a mineral water, please.
2 May I show you our wine list?		b Just oil and vinegar, please.
3 What kind of water, please?		c Medium, please.
4 What would you like to drink?		d No, thanks. We'll stay with non-alcoholic.
5 Which kind of dressing would you like?		e No, thanks. We're all full to the top!
6 Would you like a dessert?		f Still, please.
7 Would you like a starter?		g Yes, please. We're ready now.
8 Would you like to order now?		h Yes, please. I'd like a small salad.

2 ODD WORD OUT

›› SB page 16, text

Which word does not fit? Use the words in the box to say why.

alcoholic drink | dessert | fish | fruit | meat | non-alcoholic/soft drink | nut | potato product | starter | vegetable

1 lamb cutlet | rump steak | scampi | schnitzel

The odd word out is ______________ because this is ______________ and not ______________ .

2 beer | orange juice | coke | mineral water

____

3 apples | kiwis | carrots | oranges

____

4 crisps | fries | peanuts | wedges

____

5 chocolate pudding | fruit salad | prawn cocktail | ice cream

____

3 POSSESSIVE ADJECTIVES

›› SB page 18, exercise 4

Complete the sentences.

__________ [1] (My/I/Mine) brother lives in Los Angeles. __________ [2] (He/His/He's) wife comes from Mexico. __________ [3] (She/Her/She's) parents emigrated to the USA when she was small. They have __________ [4] (they/there/their) own restaurant. __________ [5] (It's/It/Its) name is "The Mexican TacAway". The meals are big and not expensive, so you really get a good deal for __________ [6] (you/your/you're) money. When we go to visit them it's __________ [7] (we/us/our) favourite place to eat!

4 COUNTABLE AND UNCOUNTABLE NOUNS

›› SB page 19, exercise 5

Complete the sentences with *a/an* or *the*, only if necessary. If you don't need an article, write ___x___ .

1 Do you want ________ ketchup on your chips?
2 Are you going to have ________[1] starter? – No, thanks. I think I'll just have ________[2] main course and then ________[3] dessert.
3 I love ________[1] ham and ________[2] eggs for ________[3] breakfast.
4 I hate ________[1] honey. I much prefer ________[2] bread and ________[3] butter with ________[4] jam.
5 I'm really full. I've just had ________[1] donut and ________[2] cappucino.
6 I'm going to buy ______ hamburger. I'm starving!

5 UNCOUNTABLE NOUNS

›› SB page 19, exercise 5

Complete the shopping list.

a ___*bit/piece*___ of cheese	a ______________ of butter
two ______________ of chocolate	six ______________ of toilet paper
a ______________ of ketchup	two ______________ of peas
three ______________ of jam	a large ______________ of ice-cream
two ______________ of bread	a ______________ of toothpaste

6 UNCOUNTABLE NOUNS AND SINGULAR VERBS

›› SB page 19, exercise 5

Complete the sentences. Use the English translation of one of the words in box A and the correct form of one of the verbs in box B.

A Beweise | Informationen | Forschung | Möbel(stücke) | Rat(schläge) | Software

B be | come | cost | look | prove | show

1 The ______________________________ that the thief was a woman.
2 Her ______________________________ direct from the president herself.
3 Her ______________________________ based on her own experience.
4 The latest ______________________________ that the weather is getting warmer.
5 The new ______________________________ twice as much as the old software.
6 Her ____________________ really ________ out of date.

7 SOME, ANY

›› SB page 20, exercise 6A

Fill in *some* or *any*.

1 **A** Would you like ______[1] chips, Tom? **B** No, thanks. I never eat ______[2] fried food.

2 **A** Jasmin, could you give me ______[1] help in the kitchen, please? **B** Just a minute. I'm just getting ______[2] carrots from the garden.

3 **A** Have you got ______[1] mustard? **B** Well, we did have ______[2] somewhere, but I can't find it now. I can borrow ______[3] from our neighbour, if you want.

4 **A** I haven't got ______[1] milk left. **B** OK, I'll go to shop and get ______[2] .

8 SOMETHING/ANYTHING, SOMEBODY/ANYBODY, SOMEWHERE/ANYWHERE

›› SB page 20, exercise 6B

Cross out the incorrect form.

1 Is Cathy ill? She hasn't eaten anything / ~~something~~ all day.

2 It's awful. I must have left my coat anywhere / somewhere [1] in town. I can't find it anywhere / somewhere [2].

3 **A** Something / Anything [1] must have happened to John. He never comes home late without phoning me. **B** I don't think something / anything [2] has happened to him. I think he's forgotten his mobile. I saw it somewhere / anywhere [3] a minute ago.

4 I've never heard anything / something so silly in my whole life!

5 I'm sorry. Ask anybody / somebody [1] else. I don't know anything / something [2] about computers.

6 **A** I read anywhere / somewhere [1] that sugar makes you stupid. **B** Yes, anybody / somebody [2] told me that, too. I hope he wasn't trying to tell me anything / something [3] because I was eating an ice-cream at the time!

9 MUCH, MANY, A LOT OF / PLENTY OF

›› SB page 21, exercise 6C

Cross out the incorrect form.

1 Hurry up, Lisa. We don't have ~~many~~ / much time.

2 How many / much TV does Harry watch a day?

3 Tom's new bike cost a lot of / much money.

4 Why did you buy so many / much [1] rolls? We have many / plenty of [2] bread already.

5 Did you see many / much people you know at the concert?

6 You needn't fill up the car. There's much / plenty of [1] petrol in the tank and we don't need many / much [2] litres to go to Leeds and back.

10 (A) LITTLE, (A) FEW

›› SB page 21, exercise 6D

Fill in *(a) few* or *(a) little*.

1 Can you give me *a little* help with this, please?

2 A lot of young people have ______ interest in good food.

3 **A** Nowadays, ______[1] people can afford to eat out.

B I know. We have only sold ______[2] meals so far today.

4 **A** Don't buy too much fish. Very ______[1] people eat it. **B** OK, I'll just buy ______[2] tuna.

5 I only have ______ money with me. I'll pay with my card.

6 **A** A lot of fathers have ______[1] time for their children, I'm afraid.

B And what about working mothers? People should think about them ______[2] , too.

D Time out

1 WORKING WITH WORDS

›› SB page 22, text

Replace the words in brackets with a synonym from the box.

agrees with her parents | are against | attitude to | chance | details | exciting place | go to | planning to get a job | points out | sad | sensible | thinks

Holly's email gives us ________[1] (information) about her future plans. She wants to go to an ________[2] (exotic destination) like Brazil or India, but her parents ________[3] (won't agree to) this idea. Holly is ________[4] (unhappy) about her parents' ________[5] (opinion of) her plans. She ________[6] (feels) that she'll never have another ________[7] (opportunity) to ________[8] (visit) such places again. But Jala ________[9] (thinks that her parents are right). She ________[10] (says) that as Holly is ________[11] (going to work) for some of the time, it would be more ________[12] (reasonable) to go to an English-speaking country.

2 THE *WILL* FUTURE

›› SB page 24, exercise 4

Fill in the correct form of the *will* future.

1 **A** I hope it ________[1] (not rain) tomorrow. **B** Well, the forecast said it ________[2] (be) cloudy but dry.

2 ________ (you + help) me with my luggage, Tom? It's heavy.

3 I must go now or I ________ (miss)[1] my plane and then I ________[2] (be) in real trouble.

4 Don't worry, Mum. I ________[1] (not forget) to phone you as soon as I land in New York. I ________[2] (call) you on your mobile so you ________[3] (not need) to wait at home.

5 How long ________ (your flight + take), Holly?

6 Drive carefully or I ________ (never lend) you my car again, OK?

3 THE *GOING TO* FUTURE

›› SB page 24, exercise 4

Fill in the correct form of the *going to* future.

1 Holly's parents ________ (visit) her in the USA soon.

2 I ________ (arrange) my time out in the USA through Work America.

3 ________ (you + work) in the USA, Holly?

4 Most of my friends ________ (not take)[1] time out. They ________ (start)[2] work immediately.

5 ________ (Holly + have) time to see the sights?

6 Hurry up! Your plane ________ (take off) in a minute.

4 WHICH FUTURE FORM?

›› SB page 24, exercise 4

Cross out the incorrect form.

1 Are you going to go / Do you go to Holly's farewell party?

2 Is Holly really going to take / Does Holly really take time out?

3 I expect I 'm / 'll be [1] a bit late, I'm afraid. You 're having to start / 'll have to start [2] without me.

4 I hope we 're seeing / 'll see Josh and Janna at Holly's party

5 The mechanic told me that he 's finishing / 'll finish fixing the car by 5 o'clock.

6 Slow down! Can't you see that the cars in front are going to stop / will stop?

5 PRESENT PROGRESSIVE WITH FUTURE MEANING

›› SB page 24, exercise 4

Josh and Janna are talking about their plans for next weekend. Fill in the gaps in their conversation.

Janna: What ____________________ [1] (you + do) at the weekend, Josh?

Josh: I ____________________ [2] (you + go) to see my sister in Brighton.

Janna: Oh, yes. ____________________ [3] (go) alone?

Josh: No, my parents ____________________ [4] (come) with me and my brother ____________________ [5] (meet) us there, too. And what about you, Janna. ____________________ [6] (do) anything?

Janna: Well, I ____________________ [7] (not do) anything special. I ____________________ [8] (stay) at home because my mum and dad ____________________ [9] (visit) some friends in Oxford at the weekend.

Josh: Hey, that sounds good! I've just changed my mind. I ____________________ [10] (not go) to Brighton after all. I ____________________ [11] (spend) the weekend here with you.

6 TRAIN TIMES

›› SB page 24, exercise 4

Look at the timetable and complete the questions and answers.

	Abfahrt		Ankunft
Frankfurt (M)	6:00	Paris	9:50
Frankfurt (M)	9:01	Paris	12:49
Frankfurt (M)	13:01	Paris	16:50
Frankfurt (M)	19:01	Paris	22:53
Paris	6:58	Frankfurt (M)	10:58
Paris	9:09	Frankfurt (M)	12:58
Paris	13:09	Frankfurt (M)	16:58
Paris	19:05	Frankfurt (M)	22:58

TGV – train à grande vitesse
Paris-Est – Saarbrücken – Kaiserslautern – Mannheim – Frankfurt a. M.

1 What time does the first train to Paris ____________________ (leave) Frankfurt?
The first train to Paris ____________________ Frankfurt at ____________________ .

2 What time ____________________ (last train / Paris / arrive) in Frankfurt?
The ____________________ in Frankfurt at 22:58.

3 Where ____________________ (train / stop) inside Germany?
The train stops at ____________________ .

4 How long ____________________ (journey / take)?
The journey ____________________ .

Shopping

1 PUZZLE

›› SB page 26, text

Do the puzzle to find the key word.

1 2 3 4 5 6 7 8 9 10 11

1 The people who serve you in a shop are the sales ... .
2 An Italian fashion designer whose name begins with A is ... .
3 Can't you take "No" for an answer? Don't be so ... .
4 Sharon's love of fashion and ... got her into debt.
5 Sharon did most of her shopping at eBay and at ... shops.
6 Another word for "shop" is "...".
7 Unfortunately, Sharon spent much more ... than she had.
8 I bought this shirt at half price. It was a real ... .
9 With designer clothes, the ... is often on the outside.
10 Sharon bought a ... cocktail dress on eBay.
11 A line of people waiting to be served is called a ... .

The key word is ____________________ .

2 ADJECTIVES

›› SB page 28, exercise 3

Find adjectives in the headlines below that match these German words.

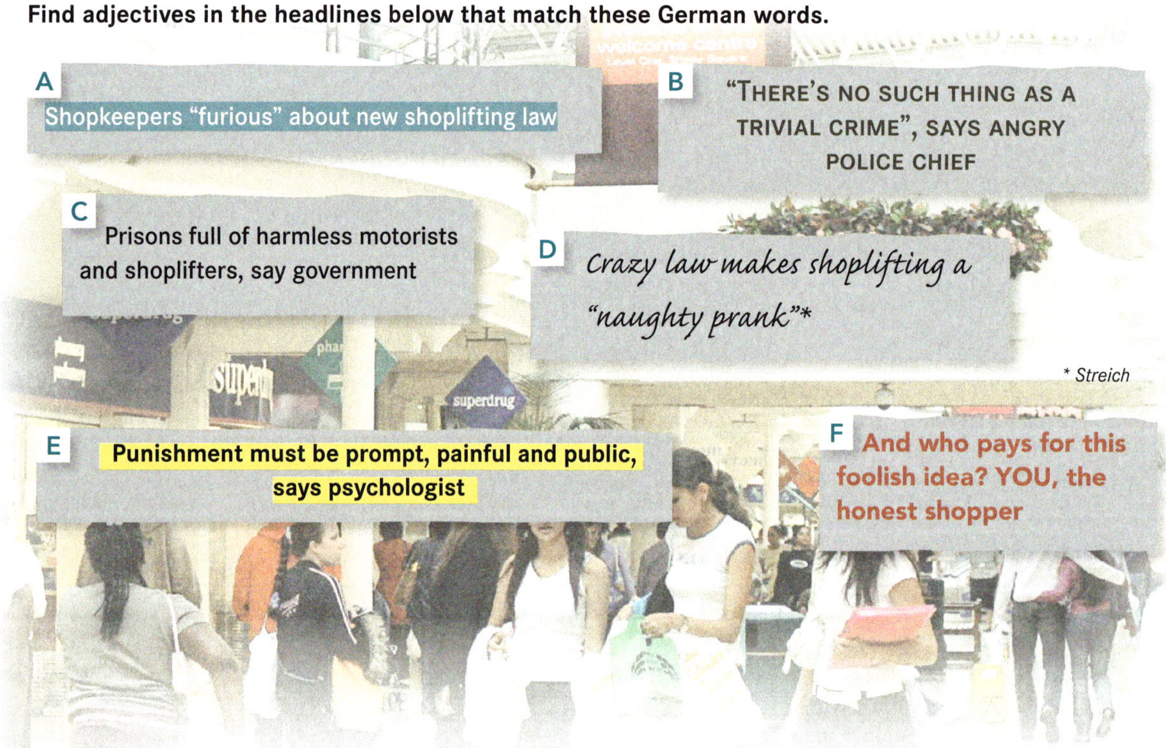

A Shopkeepers "furious" about new shoplifting law

B "THERE'S NO SUCH THING AS A TRIVIAL CRIME", SAYS ANGRY POLICE CHIEF

C Prisons full of harmless motorists and shoplifters, say government

D *Crazy law makes shoplifting a "naughty prank"**

* *Streich*

E **Punishment must be prompt, painful and public, says psychologist**

F **And who pays for this foolish idea? YOU, the honest shopper**

1 albern ____________
2 ehrlich ____________
3 erbost ____________
4 geringfügig ____________
5 harmlos ____________
6 neu ____________
7 öffentlich ____________
8 schmerzhaft ____________
9 ungezogen ____________
10 verrückt ____________
11 voll ____________
12 wütend ____________

3 ADVERBS

›› SB page 28, exercise 3

Rewrite the sentences. Use an adverb instead of an adjective.

1 Ali's English is very good. Ali speaks English very ______________________.
2 Madison is a wonderful dancer. Madison ______________________.
3 Simon is a fast runner. Simon ______________________.
4 Helen is a careful driver. Helen ______________________.
5 Accidents are always unexpected. Accidents always happen ______________________.
6 Most people are hard workers. Most ______________________.
7 Susan is a skillful painter. Susan ______________________.
8 Jim is very bad at dancing. Jim ______________________.

4 WHEN TO USE ADJECTIVES AND ADVERBS

›› SB page 28, exercise 3

Read the example sentences 1–6, then link them to the explanations a–f.

Example sentences		Explanations
1 Emma bought an exclusive dress on eBay.	c	a adjective qualifies *be/become/seem*
2 A lot of people are worried about money.		b adjective qualifies *feel/look* (= aussehen)/ *smell/taste*
3 The assistant smiled very pleasantly.		c adjective qualifies noun
4 The man looked closely at the phone.		d adverb qualifies adjective
5 This jacket is unusually good value for money.		e adverb qualifies adverb
6 Your perfume smells fabulous.		f adverb qualifies verb

5 TRANSLATION

›› SB page 29, exercise 4

Finish translating the sentences into English. Be careful about adverb order, too.

1 *Ich fühlte mich fürchterlich. Ich war fürchterlich müde.*

I felt ______________________. I was ______________________.

2 *Gewöhnlich hat sie ein ruhiges Leben. Gestern aber hatte sie ein ungewöhnliches Erlebnis.*

She ______________________.

But yesterday ______________________.

3 *Plötzlich hörte der Hund etwas. Das plötzliche Geräusch weckte ihn auf und er bellte los.*

The dog ______________________ something. The ______________________

______________________ and he began to bark.

4 *Die Musik war so laut, dass die Gäste sehr laut miteinander reden mussten.*

______________________ that the guests ______________________

______________________.

Ready for a job?

1 PHOTOS

›› SB page 30, questionnaire

Which questions in the questionnaire do the photos illustrate? Be careful: one photo doesn't fit at all.

1 ______

2 ______

3 ______

4 ______

5 ______

6 ______

7 ______

8 ______

2 JOBS

›› SB pages 30–32

Sort the jobs (box A) and the usual places of work (box B) into the correct column.

A baby-sitter | building worker | waiter | car-washer | cashier | courier rider | shop assistant | delivery boy/girl | dog-exerciser | gardener | kitchen help | shelf-filler

B building site | garage | garden | local park | private home | restaurant | self-service store | shop | street

indoor job	usual place of work	outdoor job	usual place of work
baby-sitter	*private home*		

3 PRESENT PERFECT

›› SB page 33, exercise 6

Use *has/have*, the correct form of the full verb or both.

1 Have you ______[1] (hear)? The Greens have just ______[2] (buy) a luxury caravan.

2 Have you ______ (switch) off the lights?

3 How long ______ Ben ______ (know) his girlfriend?

4 ______ the dog ______ (have) his walk yet?

5 Jack ______[1] (leave) school and ______[2] (get) a job.

6 We ______ just ______ (start) a new English book.

4 FOR, SINCE

›› SB page 34, exercise 6B

Put in *for* or *since*.

1 ____________ two years
2 ____________ she had a baby
3 ____________ 2007
4 ____________ a long time
5 ____________ ages
6 ____________ we moved to London
7 ____________ several hours
8 ____________ ever

5 THERE'S STILL WORK TO DO

›› SB page 33, exercise 6

Look at the drawings and say what the people still haven't done or haven't done yet. Be careful about word order.

1 I ____________ the washing-up ____________ .
2 We ____________ the car.
3 They ____________ the cat ____________ .
4 Susan ____________ the grass.
5 Kevin ____________ face ____________ .
6 Tom ____________ his homework.

6 SPOT THE MISTAKE

›› SB page 33, exercise 6

Cross out the incorrect form.

1 I 've lived / live here all my life.
2 We 've gone / went to the movies last night.
3 I'll help you when I finished / 've finished these emails.
4 Josh has cut / cut the grass yesterday.
5 Did you see / Have you seen Josh anywhere?
6 Susan still didn't phone / hasn't phoned.
7 I don't speak / haven't spoken to Holly for a long time.
8 Mum has told / tells you not to do that dozens of times.

7 TRANSLATION

›› SB page 33, exercise 6

Translate the sentences into English.

1 *Mein Kumpel hat eine neue Gitarre gekauft.*

My mate ____________ .

2 *Wir wohnen seit fünf Jahren in Deutschland.*

We ____________ .

3 *Hast du den neuesten Tom Hanks-Film gesehen?*

____________ latest Tom Hanks ____________ ?

4 *Ich habe meine Großeltern seit Weihnachten nicht mehr besucht.*

I ____________ .

1 Main Course
City lights

1 PREPOSITIONS

›› SB page 37, text

Stefan has arrived in New York and is emailing an American friend.
Cross out the incorrect prepositions.

Hi Paul

Well, here I am on / at / in [1] New York, and very soon I'll be seeing you in / on / at [2] Chicago. I'm looking forward at / to / into [3] that a lot!

I'm staying by / with / at [4] my cousin Krystal to / at / on [5] her little place on / up / at [6] the 11th floor in / at / of [7] an old apartment building near / under / over [8] Brooklyn Bridge.

Take a look at / into / by [9] the photo attachment. That's Krystal in / at / on [10] the right. I took the photo yesterday when we went on / by / up [11] the Empire State Building. The view through / down / over [12] Manhattan from / across / in [13] the top was fantastic! Thinking about / on / into [14] my trip to see you, I've been checking times and prices by / on / in [15] the internet, and I've decided to travel through / by / on [16] train, and I want to take the 06.45 at / in / on [17] Saturday. It'll get there at / in / on [18] 15.55. Will you be able to meet me on / through / at [19] the station?

Anyway, I must run now. Krystal and I are going to a party this evening, and she's going to introduce me with / to / around [20] all her friends.

See you soon. Stefan

2 BUILDING SKILLS: USING YOUR OWN WORDS

›› SB page 40, text

A Complete the tables with words from the Section B text.

Verb	Noun
breathe	______
______	exploration
construct	______
fail	______
recover	______

Noun	Adjective
distance	______
______	traditional
______	energetic
______	technological
______	free

B Use related words from A to rewrite the sentences, replacing the highlighted words.

1 In many New York neighbourhoods, street festivals are traditional.

In many neighbourhoods, there's a ______________________ of street festivals.

2 New York began constructing skyscrapers in the 1880s.

The ______________________ in New York began in the 1880s.

3 In the 1970s, New York failed to control drugs and crime.

In the 1970s, there was ______________________.

4 The city took quite a long time to recover after that period.

After that period, the city's ______________________.

5 Many immigrants to New York feel they are free to start life again.

Many immigrants to New York feel they have ______________________.

3 COMPARISON OF ADJECTIVES

›› SB page 44, Grammar checkpoint

Ricky wants to buy a car, but he can only buy a cheap one. Study the table and complete his thoughts.

	Chico (1.2 petrol)	Star (1.5 petrol)	Delta (1.4 diesel)
fast	*	**	***
light	***	*	**
safe	*	**	***
expensive	*	**	***
economical	**	*	***
comfortable	*	**	***
powerful	*	***	**

(*** = most; * = least)

A Complete Ricky's thoughts about the Delta.

If I have to choose one of these cars, I'd better pick the 1.4-litre Delta. It's *the most expensive*[1] (expensive) option, but with its diesel engine it's ______________[2] (economical) to run. It isn't *as powerful as*[3] (powerful) the Star. On the other hand, it's ______________[4] (fast) than the Star because it's ______________[5] (light). It's also ______________[6] (safe) of all three cars, and it's ______________[7] (comfortable), too.

B Complete Ricky's thoughts about the Chico.
(Note that some of the adjectives are the opposites of ones in the table.)

The car that I certainly wouldn't choose is the 1.2-litre Chico. Although it's ______________[1] (cheap) of the three, it isn't ______________[2] (economical) the Delta. What's more, think about all the bad points. Because it's ______________[3] (light) of the three, it's also ______________[4] (dangerous) of them all. In an accident, it would just fall to pieces! And its small 1.2 engine makes it ______________[5] (slow) and ______________[6] (powerful) of all three cars. It's also ______________[7] (comfortable) of them all.

4 TOO … AND (NOT) … ENOUGH

›› SB page 44, Grammar checkpoint

It is summer, and Ricky wants to drive his 'new' car to Oregon and see Sue. (They are still good friends!) But his parents are not happy.

Mother: listen, that car (be) / old to drive across America

Listen, that car is too ____________________

____

____________________.

Father: yes, the car (not be) tough / to go all that way

Yes, the car isn't ____________________.

Mother: I agree: it (not be) reliable / for such a big trip

____

____

Father: I really think Oregon (be) / far for this old vehicle – and for you

____

____

Mother: yes, you (be) / young for something like this

____

____

Father: yes, you (not be) experienced / a journey across the USA

____

____

Mother: and think about the cost of fuel: it (be) / expensive now

____

____

Father: yes, ancient cars like this one (not be) economical /

____

____

5 PROBLEMS WITH COMPARISONS

›› SB page 44, Grammar checkpoint

Cross out the mistake in each sentence and write the correct word(s).

1 Is NY bigger ~~as~~ Berlin? *than*
2 New York is the most amazing city of the world. ____________________
3 Manhattan is the famousest island in the world. ____________________
4 San Francisco isn't as big like New York. ____________________
5 Is San Francisco's Golden Gate Park so large as Central Park? ____________________
6 Fifth Avenue isn't the same like the other streets of Manhattan: it is very special! ____________________
7 The Brooklyn Bridge is more old than the Golden Gate Bridge. ____________________

6 WORDFIELD: CITY LIFE

A Find 18 words in the word square.

S	A	P	A	R	T	M	E	N	T	W	S	K	Y	L	I	N	E	I	K	L	M	P	O	S
C	W	K	K	L	E	Z	T	R	A	S	S	B	G	M	J	S	H	O	P	P	I	N	G	K
O	X	N	N	E	I	G	H	B	O	U	R	H	O	O	D	S	T	B	K	E	P	T	H	Y
M	S	C	W	O	I	G	P	R	E	N	Y	U	L	Q	D	C	H	U	Y	T	Z	F	B	S
M	W	A	D	H	A	T	T	R	A	C	T	I	O	N	K	R	M	I	O	R	I	E	L	C
U	C	P	N	B	M	T	W	V	X	K	V	C	B	R	U	O	L	L	N	A	B	S	T	R
N	E	I	Z	O	B	E	D	O	W	N	T	O	W	N	I	W	O	D	M	F	P	T	K	A
I	M	T	I	R	I	N	R	G	H	T	J	K	Y	E	U	D	E	I	G	F	J	I	R	P
T	K	A	L	O	R	E	M	B	U	S	I	N	E	S	S	E	Z	N	O	I	U	V	N	E
Y	P	L	W	U	E	R	V	I	O	M	Z	R	K	T	N	D	R	G	M	C	E	A	W	R
J	T	E	I	G	F	G	H	C	U	L	T	U	R	A	L	A	W	A	E	H	D	L	I	N
M	A	S	G	H	E	Y	T	P	F	I	O	N	T	W	G	T	R	A	D	I	T	I	O	N

B Now complete the following sentences with words from the word square.

1 New York is not the ______________________ of New York State; that is Albany.

2 New York has five ______________________ : Manhattan, the Bronx, Queens, Brooklyn and Staten Island.

3 The Empire State ______________________ [1] is one of the most famous ______________________ [2] in New York.

4 The Statue of Liberty is a popular tourist ______________________ .

5 The streets in Manhattan are ______________________ [1] day and night with ______________________ [2] . It takes hours to drive anywhere.

6 There is a very large Chinese ______________________ in Chinatown.

7 FURTHER OPTIONS

›› SB page 43

What does each word mean in context in the adverts (SB page 43)? Tick the correct box.

1 heavyweight
- a ☐ a large fighter, e. g. a boxer
- b ☐ an important person who other people listen to carefully

2 small screen
- a ☐ a small cinema at the Music Box Theater
- b ☐ television

3 sensation
- a ☐ an event or a person that causes much excitement
- b ☐ a strange feeling

4 rates
- a ☐ amounts or levels of payment
- b ☐ speeds at which things happen

5 seniors
- a ☐ people in higher positions than others, e. g. managers
- b ☐ older people who have come to the end of their working lives

6 performance
- a ☐ how well a person, machine, etc, does a piece of work or activity
- b ☐ a show of singing, acting, dancing, etc, for other people to watch

2 Main Course
Advertising

1 OPPOSITES

›› SB page 46, text

A Find opposites of the following in the text.

1 past ____________
2 offline ____________
3 complicated ____________
4 no-one ____________
5 shrinking ____________
6 end ____________
7 excluding ____________
8 separately ____________

B Use pairs of opposites from A to complete the following.

1 After you've found the material you need on the internet, you don't need to stay ____________[1]. You can download it and work on it ____________[2].

2 People are reading newspapers less these days, so sales are ____________[1]. However, use of newspaper websites is ____________[2].

3 "____________[1] will be at the office at 6.30 a.m.," I thought. But I was wrong. When I arrived, ____________[2] was already there!

4 The bill for the campaign came to £2.3m, ____________[1] media costs, but ____________[2] tax. That was an extra £400,000!

2 PAST PROGRESSIVE AND SIMPLE PAST

›› SB page 54, Grammar checkpoint

Make sentences with the correct form of the verbs.
Use *when* with 'short' actions.
Use *while* with 'long' actions.

The journey to Ibiza

1 / sun (rise) / Mandy (get) taxi / airport – *when*

The sun was rising when Mandy got a taxi to the airport.

2 everything / (go) well / suddenly (have) a puncture (*= Reifenpanne*) – *when*

____

3 / (look) at her watch / taxi driver (change) the wheel – *while*
She was going to be late!

____

4 / (start) again / roads (get) very busy with the morning rush hour – *when*

____

____

5 they (call) / flight for / last time / she finally (check in) – *when*

____

6 / (run) to / gate / (see) her friend Alice by / gate and (wave) – *while*

____

7 / (still explain) her terrible journey / they (get) on the plane – *when*

____

8 And that was not the end of it! / (fly) into a terrible storm / they (come down) to land in Ibiza – *while*

____

9 / (wait) for a bus / their hotel / (get) wet and cold in / rain – *while*

____

10 But thank goodness! / sun (come out) / they (drive) / the hotel – *while*

____

And it stayed warm for the whole of their holiday.

3 RELATIVE CLAUSES AND CONTACT CLAUSES

›› SB page 54, Grammar checkpoint

Complete these parts of classified ads in a local newspaper. Add *who*, *which* or *that* only where necessary. If unnecessary, write X.

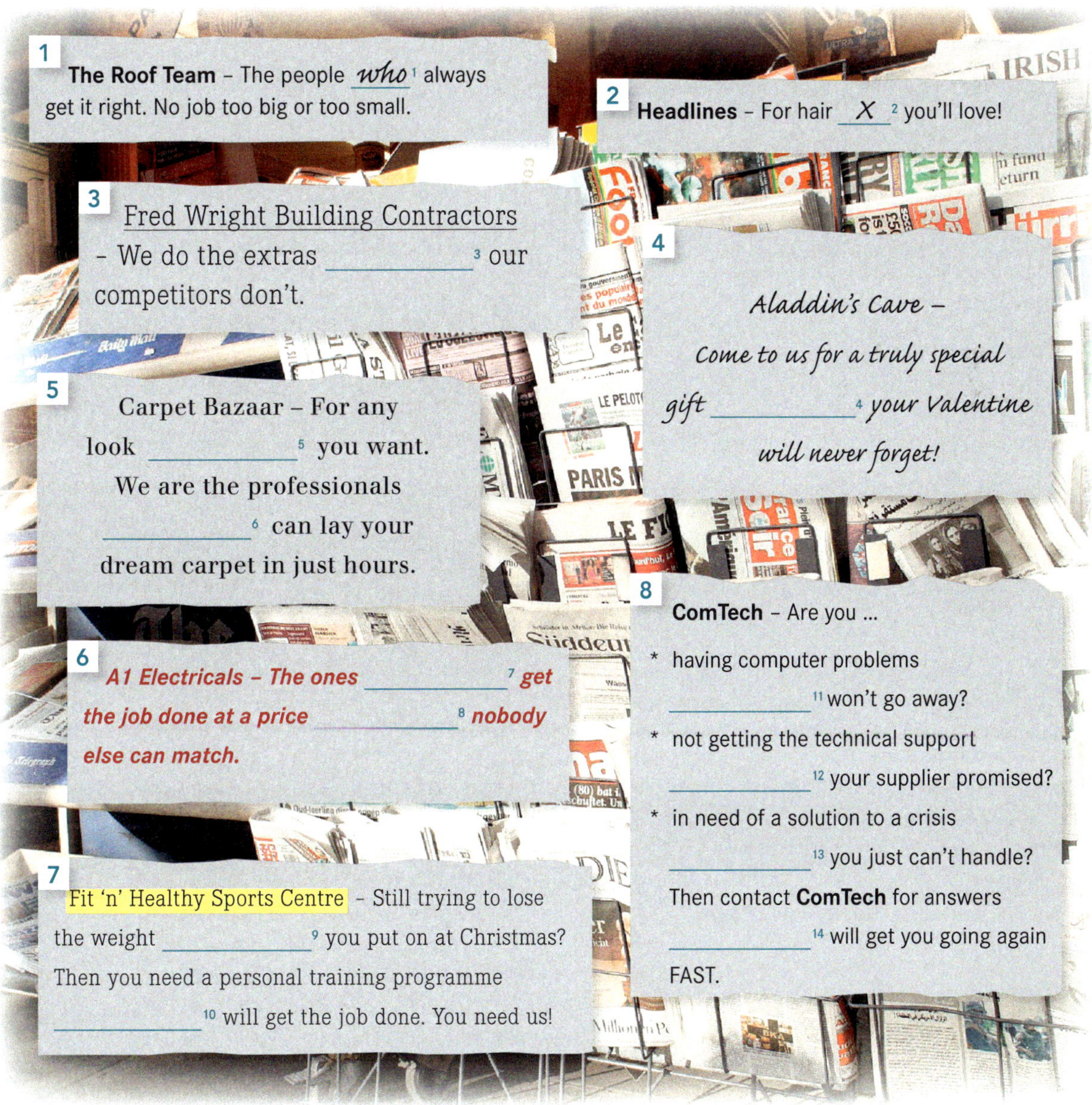

1 **The Roof Team** – The people *who* [1] always get it right. No job too big or too small.

2 **Headlines** – For hair *X* [2] you'll love!

3 Fred Wright Building Contractors – We do the extras ________ [3] our competitors don't.

4 *Aladdin's Cave – Come to us for a truly special gift ________ [4] your Valentine will never forget!*

5 Carpet Bazaar – For any look ________ [5] you want. We are the professionals ________ [6] can lay your dream carpet in just hours.

6 ***A1 Electricals – The ones ________ [7] get the job done at a price ________ [8] nobody else can match.***

7 Fit 'n' Healthy Sports Centre – Still trying to lose the weight ________ [9] you put on at Christmas? Then you need a personal training programme ________ [10] will get the job done. You need us!

8 **ComTech** – Are you ...

* having computer problems ________ [11] won't go away?
* not getting the technical support ________ [12] your supplier promised?
* in need of a solution to a crisis ________ [13] you just can't handle?

Then contact **ComTech** for answers ________ [14] will get you going again FAST.

4 BUILDING SKILLS: ANALYZING CHARTS

A Look at the chart, read the analysis and name the country:

____

GDP rose steadily between 2002 and 2004. Then there was a slight decline from 2004-2006. Following that, it remained flat in 2006-7 before a sharp rise during 2008.

B Rewrite the analysis in A. Use alternative forms as much as you can.

There was a steady rise in GDP from 2002–2004.

After that, it declined

____

C Now write about Germany between 1996 and 2002.

____

____

____

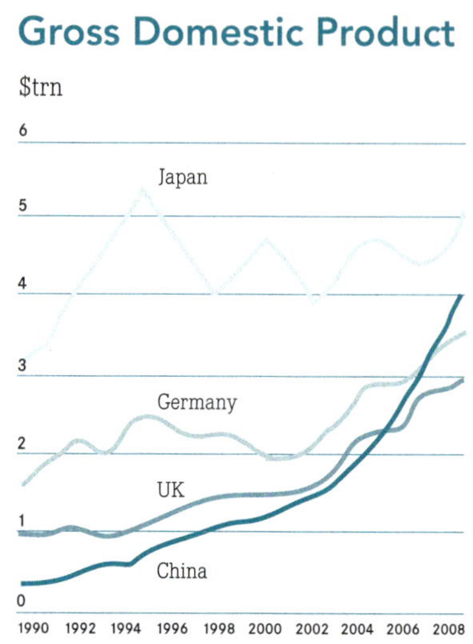

Source: *The Economist*

5 WORDFIELD: ADVERTISING

Do the crossword puzzle.

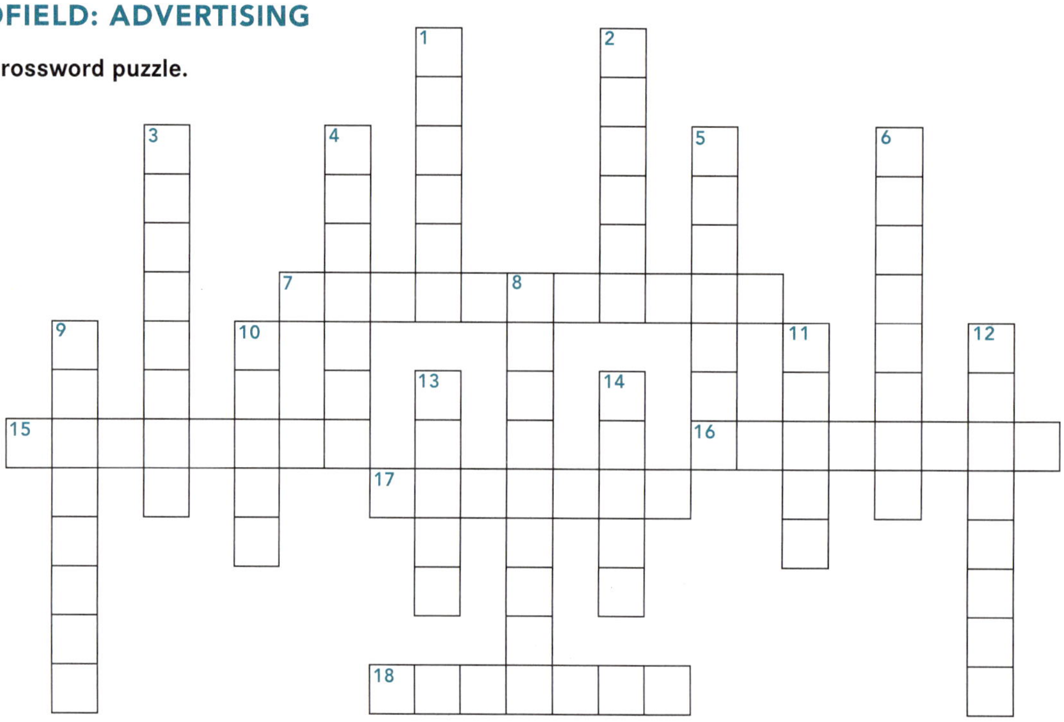

Across

7 This is the subject of Unit 2.
15 a business agreement
16 a person who makes products look their best
17 A media ... decides where and when to advertise.
18 the companies that an advertising agency works for

Down

1 You can have apple or pineapple juice. It's your ...
2 pictures
3 ... are often just made from A4 paper folded once.
4 the thing that an advertiser advertises
5 ... goods sell well because people trust the name.
6 a programme of advertising to introduce something new
8 Product placement is a clever advertising ...
9 You'll find your perfect holiday in our beautiful, new ... !
10 Look at the ... and you'll see that the company has grown fast.
11 The high ... of TV advertising make it very expensive.
12 Somebody who thinks of words or images to sell a product
13 the results of selling
14 How much money did the company ... on advertising last year?

6 FURTHER OPTIONS

›› SB page 53

A Look at the advert and analyze it in your mind, using the AIDA formula.

B Sort and expand the notes below to complete a written analysis of the AIDA process.

First of all,		attracts attention with ...
Then	the advert	raises interest through ...
After that,	the ad	creates desire by ...
Finally,	it	encourages action with ...

... simple instructions / tell you how / order / item / want
... showing actual examples / singers, songs / pictures that people will want / have
... / series of sub-headings like MUSIC RINGTONES, LOGOS / PICTURES which offer something / will interest everybody
... a picture of / attractive girl who / holding a mobile and / large headline / promises something cheap

Start like this:

First, the advert attracts attention with a ...

Media madness

1 MODAL VERBS

›› SB page 64, Grammar checkpoint

A Complete part of the conversation between Debbie, Claire, Dave and Steve on their way to the cinema. Use these forms. Sometimes more than one answer is possible.

can | can't | could | should | shouldn't | ought to

Steve: Well, which film are we going to go to?

Dave: I don't have any strong feelings, but what about the sci-fi movie? I don't know anything about it, but it ________________[1] be quite good. What do you think, Debbie?

Debbie: Well, OK, if that's what you really want ...

Claire: Well, it isn't what I want! I haven't had anything to eat since breakfast and I'm really hungry. I ________________[2] eat something before I do anything else. But *Journey to the Stars* starts at 6.30, so we ________________[3] go to a restaurant first if we go to that one.

Steve: Right. Let's forget *Journey to the Stars*. Listen, we ________________[4] go to the new *Pirates of the Caribbean*. It's great!

Claire: Oh, no! We definitely ________________[5] go to that. It's so silly! Let's go to *One Night in New York* instead. It's on at 8.30, so we ________________[6] have something to eat before it starts.

B Complete the next part of the conversation. Use each of these forms twice.

must | mustn't | needn't

Steve: OK, then. Let's go to a restaurant first and then to *One Night in New York*. Personally, I ________________[1] get home by any special time.

The only thing is this: I ________________[2] call my parents if we are going to be late.

Claire: I ________________[3] call my parents because they never worry. But I ________________[4] be home later than 11.30.

Dave: I don't have any choice. It's about the car. I ________________[5] get home late with it, or Dad won't let me borrow it again.

Debbie: And I really ________________[6] be home early because I have an important test at school tomorrow. I need my sleep!

C Now write three sentences of your own to show that you understand the difference between *must*, *mustn't* and *needn't*.

____

____

____

2 MODAL VERB SUBSTITUTES

›› SB page 64, Grammar checkpoint

A Match the modal substitutes a–d to the modal verbs 1–4.

1	d	**can/cannot:** for ability & possibility	a	do not have to
2		**can/cannot** for permission	b	have to
3		**must** for necessity	c	(not) be allowed to
4		**needn't** for non-necessity	d	(not) be able to

B Complete the sentences with appropriate modal substitutes in the correct past form.

With all his equipment in the back of the Landrover, cameraman Rob Green arrived early at the Chakragar Nature Reserve, ready for work. However, for several hours, he _had to_ [1] (*müssen*) wait at the entrance. He ________________ [2] (*nicht dürfen*) enter because he needed a special licence to film there. There was no alternative: he ________________ [3] (*müssen*) wait until the special permission arrived. At 4 p.m., the guards finally received permission to let him film in the Reserve for a week, and so he ________________ [4] (*dürfen*) enter. But because it was late in the day, he ________________ [5] (*nicht können*) start work that day, and he ________________ [6] (*müssen*) find a place to camp instead. At last, early next morning, Rob ________________ [7] (*können*) start work. He climbed and climbed and finally found the perfect place to hide with his cameras. He ________________ [8] (*nicht müssen*) wait long before the first animals arrived ...

C Now complete the sentences with appropriate modal substitutes in the correct past or *will* future forms.

His aim was to film the rare snow leopard in the wild, and this was not an easy thing to do. For the next six days, he got wonderful pictures of other animals and birds, but he ________________ [1] (*nicht können*) get the pictures that he wanted. He was very worried because by this time he was thinking, 'My one-week licence means that they won't let me stay any longer, and I ________________ [2] (*nicht dürfen*) do any more filming. So I ________________ [3] (*müssen*) go home tomorrow without any film of the leopards.' But just then, his luck changed. A leopard appeared and started chasing a deer from rock to rock down a steep cliff. Rob ________________ [4] (*nicht müssen*) do anything except turn on his camera, and he ________________ [5] (*können*) catch the whole dramatic scene on film! In the voiceover which he later added to his documentary *A Week in Chakragar*, he said, 'In a few years from now, I believe that we ________________ [6] (*nicht können*) find anything like this any more. And to see one of these amazing animals, we ________________ [7] (*müssen*) go to a zoo. Sadly, there will be none left in the wild. Not one.'

3 PROBLEMS WITH MODAL VERBS

›› SB page 64, Grammar checkpoint

Cross out the mistake in each sentence and write the correct word(s).

1 She ~~can~~ French better than Italian. *can speak*
2 We mustn't go shopping. We have everything we need. ____________
3 Last week, I must fly to New York. ____________
4 Do you can understand this book? ____________
5 You don't mustn't talk like that. It's rude ____________
6 He can't decide. He doesn't know what he will. ____________
7 I'm going to tell the assistant I would the blue coat, not the green one. ____________

4 BUILDING SKILLS: MEDIATION

›› SB page 62, exercise 6

You have a German friend who wants to join an English-language forum that discusses media news. His English is quite good, but you know that he likes to express his opinions very strongly.

You think the information on Netiquette (page 62 in your Student's Book) could help your friend. Translate paragraph 2 and the six rules to email to him.

____
____
____
____
____
____
____
____
____

5 WORDFIELD: THE MEDIA

A Find 18 words in the word square.

X	C	E	L	E	B	R	I	T	Y	T	Z	T	E	X	T	I	N	G	R	P	U	P	I	K
V	W	Q	A	J	K	L	Y	X	E	F	R	Q	A	W	E	S	R	D	C	R	V	R	N	P
I	G	P	O	P	U	L	A	R	I	G	E	M	V	I	E	W	E	R	B	E	D	O	F	R
T	M	D	S	B	M	P	L	W	L	R	A	P	L	O	K	I	J	N	M	S	U	G	H	O
I	N	T	E	R	A	C	T	I	V	E	L	R	C	O	M	E	D	Y	E	S	X	R	C	D
E	D	R	F	V	B	G	T	Z	H	N	I	U	J	I	M	O	P	Y	A	W	Q	A	E	U
Q	Y	M	O	B	I	L	E	E	S	D	T	R	T	O	F	F	L	I	N	E	U	M	F	C
M	N	B	G	V	F	V	F	E	D	C	Y	E	M	X	D	E	W	S	A	Q	I	M	D	E
D	E	D	A	U	D	I	E	N	C	E	V	R	O	M	E	S	S	A	G	E	K	E	D	R
R	F	V	B	C	D	E	S	W	X	M	U	J	V	Z	H	N	B	R	F	W	B	L	O	G
E	N	T	E	R	T	A	I	N	I	N	G	R	I	W	P	U	I	B	G	V	R	C	E	W
G	C	H	R	J	I	C	E	U	T	Z	B	Q	E	D	O	C	U	M	E	N	T	A	R	Y

B Now complete the following sentences with words from the word square.

1 *Big Brother* is an example of the sort of ______________ TV that has become very common.

2 ______________ is cheaper than making an ordinary phone call.

3 Some shows can attract an ______________ of several million.

4 For TV advertisers, each ______________ is a possible customer.

5 The TV review says the film is a ______________ , but I didn't think it was very funny!

6 As people get more and more news online and from TV, it seems that the ______________ is slowly losing readers.

7 Jessica went to India for 6 months but she kept us informed of what she was doing through a ______________ on the internet.

6 *A Week in Chakragar* is a ______________ about snow leopards.

6 FURTHER OPTIONS

›› SB page 63

A Orwell uses many adjectives to describe and lead us into the strange world of *1984*. Match the nouns in the box to the pairs of adjectives or adverb and adjective.

sky | moustache | features | face | day

1 bright cold ______________

2 heavy black ______________

3 ruggedly handsome ______________

4 harsh blue ______________

5 black-moustachio'd ______________

B Orwell uses the poster image to introduce Big Brother's heavy presence everywhere all the time. Note points from the text describing:

1 the size of the image:

... an enormous face, more than a metre wide ...

2 the number of posters in the building:

____

____

3 the number and presence of posters outside:

a ______________

b ______________

4 Big Brother's eyes, which see you everywhere and see into you:

a ______________

b ______________

4 On the move

1 *IF*-SENTENCES TYPE 1

›› SB page 74, Grammar checkpoint

Steve and Carrie are out on their new bikes and are choosing a route. Use the ideas in the picture to write their conversation.

1 **Steve:** Listen. If we go west, we'll get to Dustville. And if we go there, we'll be able to go to the concert in the park.

Carrie: Yes, but we'll have to ride through the noisy, dirty city if we do that.

2 **Carrie:** Now look, if we go north, we'll get up ____________________.

And if we go there, we'll ____________________.

Steve: Yes, but we'll ____________________.

3 **Steve:** What about this idea? If we ____________________

____________________.

Carrie: Yes, but ____________________.

4 **Carrie:** What about another idea? If ____________________

____________________.

Steve: ____________________.

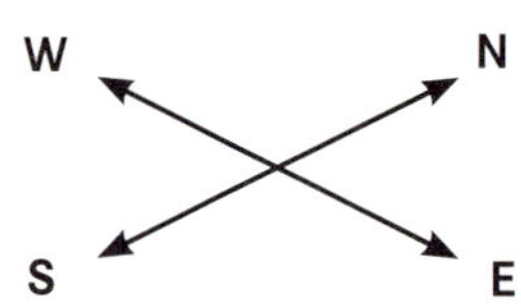

get to Dustville
for: be able to go to the concert in the park
against: have to ride through the noisy, dirty city

get up into the mountains
for: have some beautiful views
against: have to climb lots of steep hills

get into the forest
for: can have a picnic by the river
against: might get lost in the forest

get down to the beach
for: be able to go for a swim
against: get sand in all our clothes

2 *IF*-SENTENCES TYPE 2

›› SB page 74, Grammar checkpoint

Imagine that you are now on your bike at the crossroads instead of Steve and Carrie. Answer these questions with *if*-sentences type 2.

1 You are hot and want to go swimming. Which way would you go?

If I was hot and ______________________ *, I would* ______________________

2 Your gears (= *Gangschaltung*) are broken. Where would you go to find a bike shop?

If my ______________________

3 You want some photos of beautiful views across the country. Which way would you go?

____

4 You are tired and want to have a sleep somewhere cool and quiet. Where would you go?

____

3 *IF*-SENTENCES TYPES 1 AND 2

›› SB page 74, Grammar checkpoint

Read the situations. Then use the sentence parts to form *if*-sentences, types 1 or 2, as appropriate.

1 You and your friend have to catch a bus in five minutes, but he is still getting ready to go out. You say to him: we (miss) / bus / you (not hurry)

We'll miss the bus if you don't hurry.

2 However, your friend knows that there are lots of buses. He says: / we (miss) that bus, another one (soon come) and we (be able) / catch that.

____

3 Julie and Pete live and work in different cities. They cannot leave their jobs, and it is difficult for them to meet. Julie writes to him: / one of us (move), we (can be) together all the time

____

4 Pete has very little money at the moment. He writes back: / I (have) enough money, I (buy) / car, and then I (be able) / visit / more often.

____

5 Your friend is trying to choose between two cars. One is smaller and has a smaller engine. The other one is bigger and more powerful. You say to her: you (save) money on petrol / you (choose) / smaller one

____

6 You know that smaller cars are better for the environment, but you also know that a lot of people prefer faster, more powerful vehicles. You say: / everybody (buy) smaller cars, it (be) better for / environment

____

4 WORD FAMILIES

›› SB page 66, text

A Complete the table with words from Section A text lines 1–27 and words that you know or can work out. (Check your dictionary if necessary.)

Verb	Noun	Adjective *-ing* form	Adjective *-ed* form
pollute		polluting	
damage			damaged
		exhausting	exhausted
	improvement	improving	
	increase		increased

B Use words from A to complete the following.

1 *Increasing* levels of income in countries like China and India are leading to huge *increases* in the numbers of cars.

2 We live in an increasingly ______[1] environment, and we human beings are probably the ones that are causing most of the ______[2] .

3 To reduce ______[1] , we have to get older, more ______[2] vehicles off the roads.

4 Many local governments are ______[1] their public transport systems. This means fewer cars on the roads and big ______[2] in emission levels.

5 However, public transport is not perfect. Travel on Tokyo's over-crowded trains is ______[1] , and in the evening millions of ______[2] passengers fall asleep on their long journeys home.

5 WORDFIELD: TRANSPORT

Do the tree puzzle. Complete 1–9 to find and write out 10.

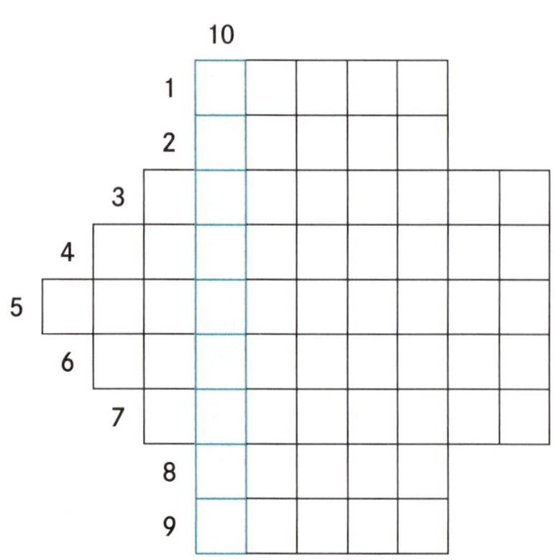

1 The government gets a lot of money from car drivers from fuel and vehicle ... .
2 Shall we take the ... through the mountains or the one along the coast?
3 In the rush hour every morning there is a three-kilometre ... along this road.
4 There wasn't much traffic on the new road at first, but quite soon it was just as ... as the old one.
5 These trains now carry 1,000 ... across the country at 300kph.
6 Prices have gone up again. Petrol is now more ... than it has ever been before.
7 Tony is a long-distance ... . He travels for three hours a day to and from work.
8 The new electric vehicles have an improved ... of up to 280 kilometres.
9 Goods leave the factory by ... and travel by road to our customers up and down the country.

10 The missing word is: ______ .

6 BUILDING SKILLS: DESCRIBING AND COMMENTING ON CARTOONS

›› SB page 68, exercise 4

A First label the sentence parts in order 1–6.

B Then label each D, A or C according to the D-A-C method: D for Describing; A for Analyzing; C for Commenting on the cartoon.

☐	☐	it also shows/passengers/helpless/ and cannot/
☐	☐	however/my opinion/not fair/attack Germain trains/this way since/
1	D	cartoon shows/station/lot/passengers who/waiting/
☐	☐	cartoon suggests/trains/often late/ unreliable
☐	☐	cartoonist may be right/trains in Britain/ America
☐	☐	near us, we/see/female passenger who looks* ... and ... as she reads/sign which directs her to/

* (See the list of adjectives on page 65 of your Student's Book.)

C Now expand the sentences to write an analysis of the cartoon in your exercise book.

This cartoon shows a station with a lot of passengers who are waiting for a ...

7 FURTHER OPTIONS

›› SB page 73

Present your choice of the two most useful features in the car on page 73 of your Student's Book. Write two short paragraphs.

One feature	that I would	probably	find really	useful	is	the	(radar).
Another development		definitely		helpful	are		(safety systems).

So if	(there were dangers ahead),	it would ...
	(I started to fall asleep),	they would ...

This	could	easily	save lives/energy/money.
	might	well	prevent accidents/waste/dangerous driving.

5 Green enough?

1 WORD PAIRS

›› SB page 80, text

A Use words from the box to form important word pairs from the text.

change | emissions | fuels | fusion | levels | power | Revolution | warming

1 Industrial ______________________
2 climate ______________________
3 sea ______________________
4 fossil ______________________
5 CO_2 ______________________
6 solar ______________________
7 nuclear ______________________
8 global ______________________

B Use word pairs from A to complete the following.

1 People are beginning to leave low-lying islands because of rising ______________________ .

2 With an average 1 °C temperature rise in the last century, ______________________ seems to be real.

3 The ______________________ began with the start of new factories in places like Manchester nearly three centuries ago.

4 For Europe, ______________________ may mean hotter summers but also wetter winters.

5 Most scientists now agree that ______________________ from human sources such as cars are helping to raise temperatures worldwide.

6 Earth receives huge amounts of energy from the sun, and many people believe that we should use this ______________________ much more than we do.

7 Most environmental problems come from our use of ______________________ – coal, gas and oil.

8 ______________________ may one day give us all the cheap, safe, clean power that we want. and so we will no longer need any of today's energy sources.

2 PAST PERFECT

›› SB page 84, Grammar checkpoint

Read the monologue from the start of another disaster movie, *When the Aliens Came*. Put the verbs in the simple past or past perfect, as appropriate. Use the past perfect when both tenses are possible.

At first, as I slowly woke up *woke up* , (wake up), I *did not know* (not know) how long I *had lain* (lie) there in that cave high in the mountains. However, I soon ______________________ [1] (realize) that I ______________________ [2] (be) there for many hours. I ______________________ [3] (arrive) there in the heat of the morning, but looking out, I ______________________ [4] (see) the last of the evening sun. I ______________________ [5] (think) about the people that I ______________________ ______________________ [6] (leave) in the burning city that morning. Perhaps the aliens ______ 7 (kill) them all already. I ______ 8 (try) to stand up, but pain ______ 9 (shoot) through my leg. I ______ 10 (remember) that I ______ 11 (fall) badly on my way up the mountain side. Perhaps I ______ 12 (break) a bone! Suddenly, I ______ 13 (freeze) in horror: a shadow ______ 14 (fall) over the mouth of the cave. Then I ______ 15 (hear) the low humming noise that I ______ 16 (learn) to fear the previous night when the alien spaceships ______ 17 (start) to attack the city. Clearly, the aliens ______ 18 (find out) about my escape somehow, and one of their deadly spacecraft ______ 19 (follow) my path to the secret cave.

3 *IF*-SENTENCES TYPE 3

›› SB page 84, Grammar checkpoint

Use the pictures and sentence parts to write about a long-distance drive that went very wrong. Use *if*-sentences type 3. Start like this:

1 not wake up late / get up on time

If Mark hadn't woken up late, he would have ______ .

2 have time to plan / trip

If he'd got up ______ .

3 remember / check / water

______ .

4 car not break down

______ .

5 not have to push / for hours

______ .

6 not miss / party

______ .

4 BUILDING SKILLS: SUMMARIZING

›› SB page 82, exercise 4

The following sentences are mixed-up summaries of two of the films in Focus on page 75.

A Find the sentences that belong to each summary.
(Use reference words, e.g. pronouns, to help order the sentences.)

B Write out the complete summaries.

C Add the film title to each paragraph.

The story follows them through to the explosion at the last possible moment.

As it opens, we meet the Mariner (Kevin Costner), who sails the ocean alone, always searching for fresh water.

From this, we move to NASA's discovery that it is going to happen again.

This movie is set in a post-apocalyptic future world where most land is now underwater.

Attacking the three of them time after time are the evil 'smokers'.

He soon finds himself unhappily giving protection to Helen and the child Enola.

These Hell's Angels on water burn oil, smoke and generally behave badly towards everyone else.

This movie is set in the days before a huge asteroid is due to hit Earth.

To do this, Stamper has to die, but the asteroid is destroyed and Earth is saved.

This small girl unknowingly carries the secret of the route to dry land in the form of a map on her back.

The only people who can drill the necessary hole are a wild group of oil drillers led by Harry Stamper (Bruce Willis).

It opens with the information that it happened 65 million years ago and could happen again.

After many dangers, the smokers are destroyed, and the heroes find the paradise of dry land.

The only answer is a nuclear explosion deep inside the asteroid to blow it to pieces.

Title: ____________________

This movie is set in a post-apocalyptic future world where most land is now underwater.

As it opens,

____

____

____

____

____

Title: ____________________

____

____

____

____

____

____

____

5 WORDFIELD: THE ENVIRONMENT

Do the crossword puzzle.

Across
1 a situation where all systems have collapsed
3 the type of weather that an area has
4 a fuel that is not solid like coal or liquid like oil
6 Water becomes this at 0 °C.
8 energy that we need e. g. for heating, lighting and making machines work
10 to do with the regular rise and fall of the sea
12 colour; here connected with looking after the environment
13 act of joining together
14 person, place or thing that provides something that we need, e. g. energy

Down
2 the air around the Earth (or another planet)
5 to stay away from something, to prevent something from happening
7 the area of land along the edge of the sea
9 a large area of land with geographical, cultural or political differences from other areas
11 a measure of weight equal to 1,000 kilograms

6 FURTHER OPTIONS

›› SB page 83

Read the situations and do the calculations. Describe your results, using *if*-sentences types 2 and 3.

Situation 1: Andy often has a shower, which takes about 25 litres, but he also has an average of three baths a week.

1 If he changed completely to showers for the next four weeks, how much water would he save?

If he ____

____

2 If he had switched completely to showers a year ago, how much less water would he have used during the past 52 weeks?

____

____

Situation 2: Charlotte brushes her teeth twice a day, and she uses about 2.5 litres of water each time. Without leaving the water running while she brushes, this figure comes down to just half a litre.

1 If she stopped running the tap for the coming 28 days, by how much would she reduce her water use?

____

____

2 If she had turned off the tap over the last year, by how much would she have cut her consumption of water since then?

____

____

6 Main Course
Modern ways to work

1 VOCABULARY

›› SB page 85, Focus

A Complete the sentences with words from the boxes. Then add the correct job title from Focus activity 1.

challenging | customer contact | independent | regular hours | repetitive | responsible

Job title: ____________________

I like working with people and so my present job with lots of ____________________[1] is just right for me. I also like it because it's not ____________________[2]: every day is different – even though I only have to work the same ____________________[3] as the sales staff. And sometimes the problems that I have to solve are quite difficult and ____________________[4]. I have to think for myself and be quite ____________________[5]. There's nobody else to ask. It's a ____________________[6] job, too, as the company must keep people happy.

B Rewrite the sentences using the words in brackets (all from pages 85–86 in your Student's Book) instead of the underlined words.

1 I'm <u>training to be a secretary</u>. (secretarial course)

____

2 I've just <u>qualified</u> in business studies. (qualification)

____

3 I <u>sent out</u> lots of <u>applications</u> for different jobs. (apply)

____

4 <u>Friendliness</u> is an important part of the work. (friendly)

____

5 I have to do everything <u>with great accuracy</u>. (accurately)

____

6 <u>The complexity of</u> today's world of work is amazing. (complex)

____

7 My new job <u>challenges me a lot</u> in many different ways. (challenging)

____

8 <u>There is more flexibility in the area of</u> training now than there used to be. (flexible)

____

2 BUILDING SKILLS: TAKING NOTES FROM READING

›› SB page 87, exercise 2

Ed Fisher has got an interview with BSG Solar. Before his interview, Ed wants to find out about the company. Read the newspaper article and complete Ed's notes.

BSG Solar: 21 Today

BSG Solar celebrates its 21st birthday this week, and looks back on a big journey from very small beginnings.

As founder and Director of this private, family-owned firm, Barry S Good says, 'We're growing rapidly, and our story shows that it is possible to turn today's environmental worries into a real business success story.' The firm specializes in supplying and fitting solar heating systems, a popular answer to the problem of rising energy costs.

The proof of BSG Solar's success is in the figures. The company now employs 550 people in 57 centres across the south of England. This is a long way from the early days when Barry first opened as BSG Heating in Oxford with just three employees. In those days, the young business supplied and fitted traditional gas central heating systems.

BSG Solar's Head Office is in the building where Barry began. Then, it contained a workshop, a store for equipment and just a small office. Now, though, the same space contains nothing but the offices that are necessary to provide the central services that are necessary for the growing organization.

BSG SOLAR **General:**

Type of organization: ____________ Director: ____________

Head Office in: ____________ Founded: ____________

Changes:	21 years ago	Now
Staff:	____________	____________
Centres:	____________	____________
The Oxford centre:	____________	____________
Type of business:	____________	____________

3 PRESENT PERFECT PROGRESSIVE AND PRESENT PERFECT

›› SB page 94, Grammar checkpoint

Complete BSG Solar's website. Where both tenses are possible, use the present perfect progressive.

Home | News | Links | Help

BSG Solar can look back on a big success story. Here are just a few of the high points.

- The company *has just opened* ¹ (just open) a new centre in south-east London – its fifth in London and 57th across the country.
- With today's continuing energy problems, the organization *has been growing* ² (grow) especially rapidly in the last three years.
- The company ____________ ³ (supply) heating systems across the whole country since 2005.
- This year, we ____________ ⁴ (become) the UK's largest solar heating supplier.
- And as of today, we ____________ ⁵ (fit) a total of 27,573 systems.
- Not only this, but BSG Solar ____________ ⁶ (also win) several important industry prizes and awards in recent years.
- Recently, the company ____________ ⁷ (upgrade) its IT and other systems at Head Office in Oxford in order to keep up with its rapid growth.
- With this in mind, we ____________ ⁸ (look for) enthusiastic new members of staff to work in our IT and Finance Departments.

4 SIMPLE PAST AND PRESENT PERFECT

›› SB page 94, Grammar checkpoint

Complete part of Ed's interview with Barry Good at BSG Solar. Put the verbs in the simple past or present perfect.

Barry: Now, you *'ve been* 1 (be) on an IT course over at the CFE since last year, *haven't* 2 you?

Ed: That's right, Mr Good, and I ______ 3 (just/finish). I ______ 4 (take) my last exam yesterday.

Barry: Oh, right. ______ they ______ 5 (give) you your results yet?

Ed: No, not yet. But I ______ 6 (have) good grades for my course work through the year,so I think I ______ 7 (pass).

Barry: But you ______ 8 (start) at the CFE the September before last, ______ 9 you? ______ you ______ 10 (do) an IT course in your first year, too?

Ed: No, I ______ 11 (be) on an access programme to improve my general education before I ______ 12 (begin) the diploma course.

Barry: So you ______ 13 (put) yourself through two years of education as an adult, ______ 14 you?

Ed: Yes, that's right, Mr Good.

Barry: Well, I think that shows real commitment, and that's something I like to see in people who work for me!

5 WORDFIELD: WORK

Find 18 words in the words square.

Q	T	E	M	P	O	R	A	R	Y	P	S	C	T	E	C	H	N	I	C	I	A	N	X	A
R	W	E	D	C	X	S	W	A	C	L	A	A	S	D	B	N	Y	I	K	N	F	P	M	R
E	C	O	N	T	R	A	C	T	L	Q	L	Z	E	X	P	E	R	I	E	N	C	E	B	O
C	E	R	X	H	V	C	D	B	E	Y	E	Q	S	X	C	D	E	R	F	V	T	G	X	U
E	Z	E	Q	T	I	O	Z	V	R	B	S	P	R	O	D	U	C	T	I	O	N	H	Q	T
P	Y	M	S	E	T	M	N	M	K	A	P	T	E	D	L	M	N	T	Z	U	I	R	E	I
T	T	P	T	F	Z	M	U	B	S	R	E	T	W	O	R	K	P	L	A	C	E	F	E	N
I	F	L	G	A	H	I	J	E	X	F	R	D	W	E	F	T	G	Z	H	U	J	I	C	E
O	V	O	B	C	N	T	M	N	E	T	S	C	W	D	P	R	O	S	P	E	C	T	S	M
N	C	Y	Z	T	M	M	I	E	D	G	O	V	V	F	R	T	G	B	Z	H	N	Z	H	N
I	X	E	H	O	J	E	K	F	C	B	N	F	Z	I	N	T	E	R	V	I	E	W	D	C
S	Y	R	J	R	U	N	O	I	W	A	I	T	E	R	M	N	B	G	F	V	D	C	S	X
T	Q	E	M	Y	I	T	L	T	R	U	Z	U	H	N	E	M	P	L	O	Y	M	E	N	T

6 PROBLEMS WITH VERBS

Cross out the mistake in each sentence and write the correct word(s).

1 Ben ~~is taking~~ the train to college every morning. *takes* __________
2 Terry and Julia can't go out. They do their homework. __________
3 I am liking my new job more and more. __________
4 Tom didn't start college on Day 1. He travelled back from India at the time. __________
5 Annie will have a baby, so she's taking maternity leave. __________
6 Kirsty and James work here for two years. __________
7 I'm sorry, but the manager isn't here. She just go home. __________
8 Tony and Emma have been knowing each other since they did Business Studies together. __________
9 The computer doesn't start! What's wrong with it? __________
10 I would accept the job if they would offer it to me. __________

7 FURTHER OPTIONS

›› SB page 93

A Read the pieces of advice a–d from a producer of aptitude tests. Then match these pieces of advice to test types 1 and 2.

Advice	
a	Solve visual puzzles in newspapers and magazines.
b	Practise reading data from timetables, e. g. car ferry, bus or train timetables.
c	Play games that make you think about strategies and doing tasks in order, e. g. chess, solitaire.
d	Do number puzzles and read financial reports in newspapers.

How to improve your scores in aptitude tests

1 Numerical tests: ☐ ☐ 2 Diagrammatic and coded instruction tests: ☐ ☐

B Complete the sentence parts a–h then add them to the appropriate sections 1 or 2.

Advice			
a	be careful not / waste time / difficult questions	e	read each question carefully before / answer /
b	don't stay up late / night before / testing session	f	remember / leave plenty / time / get to / session
c	if / don't understand something, don't / afraid / ask	g	remember / listen carefully / all instructions
d	if / wear glasses, remember / take / with you	h	work quickly / accurately, keeping your eye on / time

How to do your best in a testing session

1 Before the session:

____

____

____

2 At the session:

____

____

____

____

____

7 Main Course
Going global

1 VOCABULARY

›› SB page 96, text; page 99, text

**A Complete Table 1 with words from the Section A text.
Complete Table 2 with words from the Section B text.**

1

Verb	Noun
globalize	________
solve	________
transmit	________
________	development
________	requirement
employ	________

2

Noun	Adjective
________	free
________	redundant
________	strong
________	weak
independence	________
competition	________

B Look at the highlighted words. Use related words from A to help rewrite the sentences.

1 With its name for reliability, the Black Cat brand has real strength.
With its name for reliability, the Black Cat brand is ________________.

2 During the last 50 years, there has been a rapid development in free trade.
During the last 50 years, free trade ________________.

3 It's the technicians' job to find a solution to the problem.
It's the technicians' job to ________________.

4 Many workers have no freedom to ask for better conditions.
Many workers ________________.

5 These days, it costs very little to transmit data electronically.
These days, electronic ________________.

2 WORDFIELD: GLOBALIZATION

Do the tree puzzle. Complete 1–9 to find and write out 10.

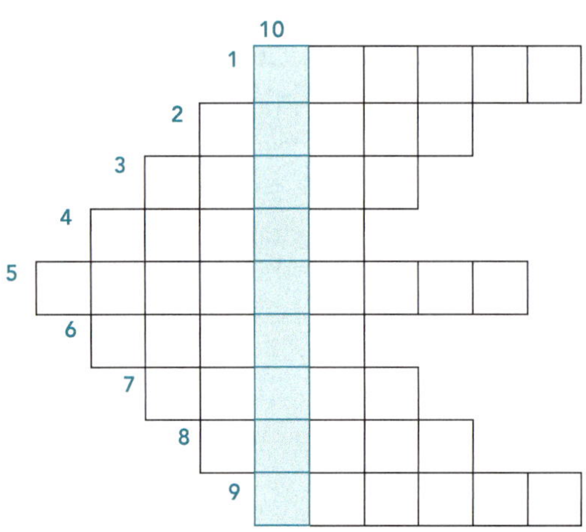

1 money that is made from selling – after paying all business costs
2 summer food from trees that is often transported round the world to be sold somewhere else in winter
3 things that are produced for sale
4 the activities of buying and selling goods or services
5 people who buy and use goods and services
6 the amount of money that you have to pay to buy something
7 describing something that is lower in price than you expect
8 a product or group of products with its own name
9 an amount of something that is available to be used

10 ________________

3 BUILDING SKILLS: WRITING A COMMENT

›› SB page 102, exercise 4

A Choose the correct connectors to complete the comment.

Comment on the following: 'People's jobs are more important than cheap goods in the shops.'

This view suggests that we should keep out cheap goods from places like China in order to protect our own industries and jobs. Because/While [1] some people strongly support this view, others are strongly against it. Let us consider some of the arguments for and against the protectionist view. On the one hand,/For example, [2] the loss of jobs causes great personal problems and huge social pressures. In addition,/On the other hand, [3] lack of competition lets protected local producers refuse to develop better products at lower prices. As a result,/Despite this, [4] the local economy slowly gets weaker and people get poorer. Moreover,/Therefore, [5] it is clear that there is no easy choice to make. For instance,/However, [6] it seems to me that ______________________________.

My main reason for saying this is that ______________________________

____

B Now add your own views in the paragraph above.

4 THE PASSIVE: DESCRIBING A PROCESS

›› SB page 104, Grammar checkpoint

Use the sentence parts to describe the car production process.

1 all/car parts (deliver)/factory just/time for use

All the car parts are delivered to the factory just in ______________________________

____

2 /parts (take) straight to/production line

____

____

3 /body (put together) separately from/rest of/car

____

____

4 then/engine and all/other parts (mount) in/body

____

____

5 at/end, everything (check) very carefully/quality controllers

____

____

6 finally,/finished cars (load) onto transporters and (distribute) all over/world

____

____

5 THE PASSIVE: QUESTIONS

›› SB page 104, Grammar checkpoint

Jack emailed his new boss Margaret Beckwith about 'Baskets of Bengal' (Grammar checkpoint, Exercise 2). Margaret has some questions. Write her email back. Put her questions in the passive.

1 *Will B of B pay Stephen Carter's travel costs?*

2 *Have you agreed travel dates with Stephen yet?*

3 *How many units are you going to order?*

4 *Will all of our shops sell this first order?*

5 *Will you place a larger order before Christmas?*

6 *We might order more baskets next year. Which shops will you ask to sell them?*

7 *I would like to use a specialist product designer at a later date. Will B of B pay for this person?*

Jack:

Re: Baskets of Bengal

Just a few questions if I may.

1 *Will Stephen Carter's travel costs be paid by B of B?*

2 ____________________

3 ____________________

4 ____________________

5 ____________________

6 ____________________

7 ____________________

6 PASSIVE WITH MODALS

›› SB page 104, Grammar checkpoint

Write Jack's reply to Margaret. Use his answers and modals in the passive.

Margaret:

In answer to your questions:

1 (Yes / have to) *Yes, Stephen Carter's travel costs have to be paid by B by B.*

2 (No / should / soon) ____________________

3 (1,000 / ought to) ____________________

4 (No / needn't) ____________________

5 (Yes / could) ____________________

6 (All shops / might) ____________________

7 (Yes / have to) ____________________

7 PROBLEMS WITH PASSIVES

›› SB page 104, Grammar checkpoint

Cross out the mistake in each sentence and write the correct word(s). (In one sentence, no words are needed.)

1 With all the new orders, extra production was requiring at the second factory. ____________

2 Bill has just offered a new job in export sales. ____________

3 Our Kenyan FAIRTRADE coffee can bought at any of our stores. ____________

4 More information about FairTrade may be found on the website by you. ____________

5 I hope the people who treat their workers so badly will be catched and punished. ____________

6 This interesting new book, *Globally Speaking*, is from the famous Dr James Ronson. ____________

7 These beautiful FAIRTRADE shirts are made from pure cotton. ____________

8 It said that the Chinese economy will one day be larger than America's. ____________

8 FURTHER OPTIONS

›› SB page 103

Read the role cards on pages 155–159 of the Student's Book (Files 4, 8, 9 and 15) then match the sentences below to the speakers.

1 New Look D

2 Gold Star

3 Mayor

4 Gold Star

5 Union

6 Gold Star

7 Union

8 New Look

A I agree to try it. To protect our own brand image, we have to take strong action in support of the workforce.

B But that happens because we are being forced by you to supply at the lowest prices.

C Your workers are highly skilled, and with our help, they're ready to fight for better pay and conditions.

D We can't be seen by our customers to allow suppliers like you to pay your workers so badly.

E If you really want their workers to win better conditions, you must force Gold Star to accept us

F This town needs your company, but our people are just not being paid enough.

G Higher wages will force New Look to find somewhere cheaper. And that would mean terrible unemployment here.

H We're not going to be pressured by any unions here. If you start causing trouble, we're going to move to another country.

8 Main Course
Finding a job in the EU

1 VOCABULARY

›› SB page 106, texts

Use one of the phrases from the box to complete the sentences.

are not paid | can make a contribution | chooses the UK | do a period | does not give the name | emails Lisa the name | is studying tourism | pay a fee to get | require students | SEC specializes in

1 Lisa ______________________ at a university in Bremen.
2 Students have to ______________________ of practical training abroad.
3 Some courses ______________________ to go to an English-speaking country.
4 Lisa ______________________ because it is similar to Germany.
5 The online agency ______________________ arranging internships abroad.
6 SEC's ad ______________________ of the host company.
7 Unfortunately, interns ______________________ a salary.
8 The host company ______________________ towards an intern's living expenses.
9 Lisa has to ______________________ full details of the internship.
10 SEC ______________________ of a contact person in Norwich.

2 BUILDING SKILLS: WRITING A CV

›› SB page 108, exercises 3–6

1 Use numbers from 1 to 6 to put Tobias Kraft's personal details into the correct order. Put a cross (X) by the two items they do not belong in this section of a CV at all.

2 Tick (✓) the items you would expect to find in the Interests and skills section of a CV, and cross (×) the items that do not belong there.

TOBIAS KRAFT

Personal details

- ☐ Daytime phone number
- ☐ Address
- ☐ Marital status
- ☐ Date and place of birth
- ☐ Email address
- ☐ Sex
- ☐ Name
- ☐ Nationality

TOBIAS KRAFT

Interests and skills

- ☐ References
- ☐ Cycling and camping
- ☐ English and Spanish
- ☐ LAN parties
- ☐ EU class C driving licence
- ☐ Martin-Luther-Grundschule
- ☐ Member Red Cross
- ☐ MS Office

3 GERUND OR INFINITIVE?

›› SB page 114, Grammar checkpoint

A Complete the table with verbs from the box.

admit | afford | ~~begin~~ | continue | deny | dislike | ~~dream of~~ | enjoy | expect | finish | hate | hope | imagine | intend | like | love | mention | practise | prefer | promise | start | stop *(unterbrechen)* | want | ~~would prefer~~

Infinitive	Gerund	Both
would prefer	*dream of*	*begin*

B Use a verb or verb form from the table + infinitive or gerund to express the ideas below. Sie möchten jemandem sagen, dass Sie …

1 … versprochen haben, rechtzeitig anzukommen.

____

2 … immer davon geträumt haben, im Ausland zu arbeiten.

____

3 … sich nicht vorstellen können, viel Geld zu gewinnen.

____

4 … es Freitagabend vorziehen würden, zu Hause zu bleiben.

____

5 … begonnen haben, Französisch zu lernen.

____

6 … anhalten müssen, um Geld zu holen.

____

4 VOCABULARY

›› SB page 112, exercise 2

Cross out the incorrect form.

1 Nowadays, most EU states recommend / ~~recommended~~ [1] that children are educated in mix / mixed [2] classes.

2 The EU is threatened / threatening [1] to break off negotiations with Romania if the country doesn't fight corrupt / corruption [2] more effectively.

3 In the fight against terrorism, western governments want to stop extremists from corrupting / corruption the minds of the young.

4 The national media is largely responsible / responsibility [1] for giving people a false perception / perceptive [2] of what the European Commission does. In fact, Brussels plays a purely advise / advisory [3] role.

5 Democratic governments can advice / advise [1] and even recommend / recommendation [2], but they have no right to interfere / interfering [3] in the private lives of their citizens.

6 This article about state interfere / interference [1] in our personal affairs is very perceive / perceptive [2]. I learnt a lot from it.

5 BUILDING SKILLS: QUALIFYING OPINIONS

›› SB page 112, exercise 3

Eric and Martin are talking about the EU. Complete their discussion with the phrases from the box

as far as I can see | I get the impression that | It is absolutely clear | On the contrary, the fact is | On the whole, I suppose that | the opposite is true | There can be absolutely no doubt | This fact seems to suggest that

Eric: I'm so fed up with European bureaucrats telling us what to do all the time. I think the EU is just a waste of taxpayers' money.

Martin: Well, ______________________________ [1], there are quite a few benefits from the EU. The EU can fight international crime better than national governments can, for example.

Eric: I don't believe that for a moment. ______________________________ [2] to me that we would be better off without the EU. Just look at all that money they spend on translating everything into all the languages.

Martin: Well, that is a problem, of course. But from listening to the news, ______________________________ [3] the politicians want to limit the number of languages used.

Eric: No, ______________________________ [4]: every country insists on having everything in its own language.

Martin: ______________________________ [5] it does cost a lot of money, but it is necessary, I think. But I'm conviced the EU does help: where would we be if people couldn't move from one country to another to get a job.

Eric: I don't really agree with you at all. ______________________________ [6] that all these people moving around the continent are just pushing down wages. ______________________________ [7] that we would have more money to spend if there weren't so many immigrants taking our jobs away.

Martin: I can't agree with you there. ______________________________ [8] the free movement of labour creates more jobs and is better for the economy.

6 WORDFIELD: WORD COMPLETION

A Put the missing vowels into the words and expressions you need to talk about the EU.

1 C _ RR _ PT _ _ N
2 _ NT _ RF _ R _ NC _
3 _ ND _ M _ CR _ T _ C
4 B _ R _ _ _ CR _ TS
5 P _ RC _ PT _ _ N
6 _ _ R _ P _ _ N C _ MM _ SS _ _ N
7 N _ T _ _ N _ L G _ V _ RNM _ NTS
8 L _ G _ SL _ T _ VE P _ W _ R
9 C _ _ NC _ L _ F M _ N _ ST _ RS
10 M _ MB _ R ST _ T _

B Complete the sentences with five of the words / expressions you have found.

1 A lot of people do not understand that the ______________________[1] has no ______________________[2] at all. It can only advise and recommend.

2 A big problem is that the ______________________[1] is made up of the heads of the ______________________[2].

3 The media is full of stories of corrupt ______________________[1] in Brussels but in fact ______________________[2] are responsible for paying out money to farmers, for example. It is all a question of ______________________[3], not reality.

7 FURTHER OPTIONS

›› SB page 113

calm | careful | cheerful | experienced | fit | friendly | fun-loving | generous | have a sense of humour | helpful | knowledgeable | mechanically/technically-minded | reliable | skilful | sociable | sympathetic | tolerant | understanding

Say what kind of person you would you like your companion(s) to be in these situations.

1 You want to go mountain-climbing. The weather is bad, and you have never been mountain-climbing before.

In this situation I'd like (to be with) a person who is calm, fit and reliable because mountain-climbing is dangerous and hard work.

2 You've been working hard lately and now you need a really good night out with a lot of fun.

In this situation ______________________

3 Your scooter won't start and you don't know why. You don't have enough money to have it repaired by a professional, so you need help from your friends.

In this situation ______________________

4 You are in hospital after a road accident. You are not badly injured but you are feeling bored and guilty because the accident was your fault. You want people to visit you.

In this situation ______________________

9 Social challenges

1 VOCABULARY

›› SB page 116, text; page 119, text

A Create opposites of these words from the Section A and B texts. Use your dictionary if necessary to help you choose from the following prefixes.

de- | dis- | il- | im- | in- | ir- | mis- | un-

Section A text

1 perfect ______
2 tidy ______
3 responsible ______
4 prove ______
5 possible ______
6 believe ______

Section B text

7 action ______
8 understand ______
9 direct ______
10 attention ______
11 use ______
12 decrease ______

B Use pairs of words from A and B to complete the following. Change their forms if necessary.

1 We need a free press to check that politicians ______[1] their power well and do not ______[2] it by acting dishonestly.

2 Parents who do not care for their children are very ______[1], and are often partly ______[2] for their children's future problems.

3 The WHO plans strong ______[1] against malaria as ______[2] would mean the deaths of millions more, including many children.

4 As many young people grow up, family influence ______[1], and peer group pressure to join gangs ______[2].

5 People often see their role models as ______[1] in every way, but role models are only human, and all humans are very ______[2].

6 Some people fail to vote because they think it is ______[1] to change society. But others feel that voting is their only ______[2] way of getting a better government.

2 PARTICIPLE CLAUSES 1

›› SB page 124, Grammar checkpoint

Join the pairs of sentences. Use the word in brackets with the correct sentence and change the following verb into an *-ing* participle.

1 You are legally allowed to gamble at casinos in the USA. You reach the age of 18. *(after)*.

You are legally allowed to gamble at casinos in the USA after reaching the age of 18.

2 Tracy Parr grew up in Sandpoint, Idaho. She learned that various family members enjoyed a little gambling. *(when)*

______

______

3 She reached her 18th birthday. She immediately drove with her boyfriend, Carl, to the nearest casino. *(on)*

4 She lost $5 – a small price for a lot of fun, she thought. She played every machine in the place that evening. *(while)*

5 She left the casino to go home that night. She had already become a gambling addict. *(before)*

6 She spent more and more time at the casino in the following months. She sometimes won but usually lost – and could never stop. *(while)*

7 She nearly went to prison. She stole money from work to feed her addiction. *(after)*

8 She thought there was no escape from gambling. She finally joined a group called Gamblers Anonymous which showed her the way out. *(before)*

3 PARTICIPLE CLAUSES 2

›› SB page 124, Grammar checkpoint

Change the relative clauses (starting with *who*, *which*, *that*) to *-ing* or *-ed* participle clauses. Rewrite the text in your exercise book.

Dr Louisa Piper is a psychologist **who is trained** as a therapist and **who now specializes** in the area of family problems. She helps family members who have difficulties in their relationships. She says the problems that face them are often caused by outside stresses. For example, she often sees parents who are forced to work very long hours to earn enough money. That can badly affect children who grow up in this lonely environment. The personal problems that are created by such pressures come in many forms. She gives as an example one family that has been badly damaged in this way. There is an 18-year-old daughter who was recently taken to hospital with severe anorexia. There is also a 15-year-old daughter who is staying out late at night and who is spending time with known troublemakers. And there is a 10-year-old son who is too frightened to leave the house at all. Piper is now setting the family challenges that are designed to bring them together. For instance, Sunday evening has become a 'fun family time' which requires them all to spend time together on a shared family activity.

Start like this:
*Dr Louisa Piper is a psychologist **trained** as a therapist and now **specializing** in the area of family problems.*

4 ARTICLES

›› SB page 124, Grammar checkpoint

Add *a/an* or *the* where necessary. Write *x* where no article is needed.

Steffie Kaufman, animal rights activist

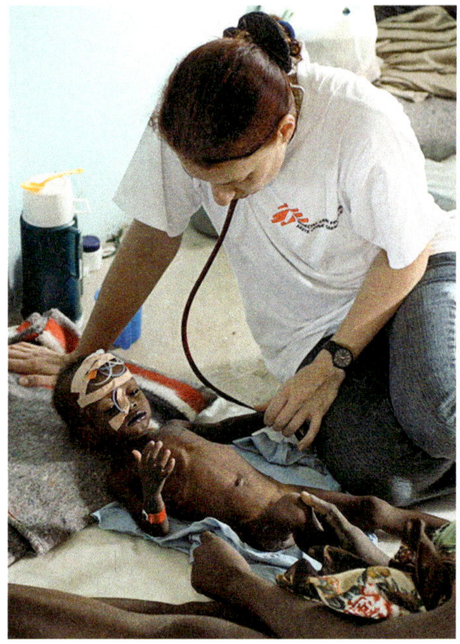

As __a__[1] child at __x__[2] school, Steffie was always very good at ________[3] science. When she was still very young, she decided that she would like to go to ________[4] college and become ________[5] doctor. However, she also loved ________[6] animals, she read all ________[7] books about ________[8] zoology that she could find, and she often wondered whether to become ________[9] vet* instead. She changed her mind ________[10] thousand times, but finally she applied to go to ________[11] medical school. However, as ________[12] student she soon became ________[13] animal rights activist, and one night she went with ________[14] group of ________[15] students to free all ________[16] animals kept for ________[17] animal experiments at the university's science laboratories. She and some of ________[18] other activists were caught by ________[19] police, and they were told to appear in ________[20] court ________[21] few weeks later. There, they were each ordered to do ________[22] hundred hours of ________[23] community service. Since getting her medical qualifications, Steffie has been working for ________[24] World Health Organization in ________[25] central Africa in the long fight to control ________[26] tropical diseases like ________[27] malaria. There are ________[28] lot of endangered animal species in that part of ________[29] world and, not surprisingly, Steffie is also doing ________[30] work in her free time to help protect species in danger such as ________[31] famous silver-back gorilla.

***vet:** short for 'veterinarian' (= *Tierarzt/-ärztin*)

5 WORDFIELD: SOCIAL CHALLENGES

A Find 20 words in the word square.

A	G	O	V	E	R	N	M	E	N	T	W	X	W	M	B	P	M	A	B	A	N	D	O	N
P	E	S	X	T	A	I	K	L	T	P	R	E	S	S	U	R	E	D	Y	N	Q	P	W	P
E	L	E	C	T	I	O	N	M	B	W	E	R	L	I	E	T	R	M	W	V	N	O	R	E
T	V	R	W	C	H	S	I	S	O	C	I	A	L	I	Z	E	G	O	E	I	P	L	S	M
R	M	E	A	N	S	T	S	G	E	R	S	P	L	C	B	N	R	V	N	O	M	I	T	O
E	D	L	U	S	D	R	A	D	D	I	C	T	I	O	N	T	X	E	C	L	Y	C	M	T
L	Y	A	P	O	L	U	V	M	W	E	K	L	E	Q	T	E	C	M	B	E	P	I	E	I
I	K	T	L	C	N	C	P	O	L	I	T	I	C	I	A	N	M	E	W	N	T	E	I	O
G	M	I	A	I	P	T	W	R	C	A	Y	Q	W	E	P	C	M	N	T	C	R	S	Z	N
I	Y	V	M	E	Y	U	N	C	A	M	P	A	I	G	N	E	L	T	S	E	W	I	E	A
O	I	E	X	T	E	R	B	R	I	D	E	Z	T	G	U	I	C	I	D	R	U	G	A	L
N	A	I	L	Y	W	E	H	G	M	E	D	I	A	O	P	L	H	E	W	O	X	K	C	L
A	C	H	I	L	D	C	A	R	E	X	N	D	E	M	O	N	S	T	R	A	T	I	O	N

B Now complete the following sentences with words from the word square.

1 Women fought a long ______________________ for the right to vote.

2 Women's traditional roles were ______________________ and making a home.

3 If a child's parents cannot look after it, this role is sometimes accepted by ______________________ such as grandparents.

4 One of today's greatest causes of social problems is drug ______________________ .

5 The job of a ______________________ is to be a strong voice for the people who voted for him or her.

6 Yesterday, there was a big ______________________ against the government. About 100,000 people came to march through the capital.

6 FURTHER OPTIONS

›› SB page 123

Here is another 'conversation poem'. This conversation takes place betwen a teacher (T) and a pupil, Blenkinsop (B). Put Blenkinsop's replies in the correct places.

a All dead, sir. b Can't do it, sir. c Can't, sir. d Dead, sir. e Grandma, sir. f Grandmothers, sir? None, sir.	g Home, sir. h I'd been looking forward to it too, sir. i I know. It's very upsetting*, sir. j My hand, sir. k No *kit, sir.	l No, sir. My teeth, sir. m Not ironed, sir. n She died, sir. o She's seriously dead all right, sir.

***kit:** clothes needed for a special activity, usually a sport; ***upsetting:** *erschütternd*

Conversation Piece

by Gareth Owen

T: Late again, Blenkinsop?
What's the excuse this time?
B: Not my fault, sir.
T: Whose fault is it then?
B: Grandma's, sir.
T: Grandma's. What did she do?
B: ______________________
T: Died?
B: ______________________
T: That makes four grandmothers this term
And all on PE days, Blenkinsop.
B: ______________________
T: How many grandmothers have you got,
Blenkinsop?
B: ______________________
T: None?
B: ______________________
T: And what about yesterday, Blenkinsop?
B: What about yesterday, sir?
T: You missed maths.
B: That was the dentist, sir.
T: The dentist died?
B: ______________________
T: You missed the test, Blenkinsop.
B: ______________________
T: Right, line up for PE.
B: ______________________
T: No such word as can't. Why can't you?
B: ______________________
T: Where is it?
B: ______________________
T: What's it doing at home?
B: ______________________
T: Couldn't you iron it?
B: ______________________
T: Why not?
B: ______________________
T: Who usually does it?
B: ______________________
T: Why couldn't she do it?
B: ______________________

10 Main Course
Multiculturalism

1 BUILDING SKILLS: DESCRIBING ILLUSTRATIONS

›› SB page 125, Focus

Use the text plan to describe the drawing of a street market on page 125 of the Student's Book in detail. Write in an exercise book. Add any other details you may see.

In the	foreground	there	is	a	boy(s)	wearing a	hijab.
	middle distance	you can	are	an	girl(s)	with	turban.
	background		see	some	children		sari.
				two	older people		jacket.
				three	younger people		jeans.
				...	old man/men		long hair.
					young woman/women		shaved head.
					black/white		
					Muslim/Sikh		

On the right	there is a	fruit stall.
On the left		grocery stall / shop.
In the middle		church / town hall.
		clock tower.
		street lamp.

A	stallholder	is	looking at	a	bag.
An	older man	are	selling	an	fruit.
The	boys		laughing	some	friends.
			carrying		shopping trolley.
			talking		customers.
			holding		
			pushing		

In the foreground in the middle there are two boys. They are laughing. There is a fruit stall on the left. Two older people are buying some fruit from the stall-holder. In the background ...

2 CONNECTORS

›› SB pages 126–127, text

Underline the correct connector.

Hanif Kureishi, who / whose [1] father is Pakistani and mother English, was born in the London suburb of Bromley. After / When [2] leaving Bromley Technical High School, he spent a year at Lancaster University before / but [3] dropping out. However / Moreover [4], he later went to London University and / but [5] got a degree in philosophy.

His first novel, called *The Buddha of Suburbia*, won a prize and / furthermore [6] was also made into a successful TV series. His next major novel, *Intimacy*, about a man leaving his wife and two young sons because / because of [7] his wife's coldness caused surprise as / while [8] Kureishi himself had recently left his wife and two young sons.

In fact / Therefore [9], the autobiographical nature of Kureishi's work caused big problems. This was because / due to [10] his family felt that he made unfair use of them in his novels by / from [11] "selling them for his own profit".

Hanif's sister, Yasmin, was particularly bitter on account of / because [12] the autobiographical content of *The Buddha of Suburbia*, in which / which [13] the Buddha is an obvious portrait of her father. Although / As a consequence [14] Yasmin wrote to a newspaper saying that her father was so angry that / therefore [15] he didn't speak to Hanif for nearly a year.

3 REPORTED SPEECH: STATEMENTS

›› SB page 134, Grammar checkpoint

Rewrite the statements for a newspaper report on illegal immigration into Spain. Use the introductory verbs in brackets.

1 

Minister: "The Spanish government is doing all it can to stop illegal immigration, but we cannot do the job alone. The rest of the EU must help us." *(tell reporters; add)*

Speaking in English, the Spanish interior minister ______________________

____

____

____

2 

Dr Sanchez: "We have found that Spain needs some skilled immigrants, but unfortunately the illegals are almost all unskilled. Most can't even understand Spanish." *(say; point out)*

Dr Sanchez, an economist, ______________________

____

____

____

3 

Julia Gonzales: "The anti-immigrant feeling in Spain has been made much worse by the media, which always exaggerates the number of people who are coming here." *(think)*

Julia Gonzales ______________________

____

____

____

4 

Priest: "People think that African immigrants just want to come to Spain to have a better life, but I see it as a humanitarian problem. The fact is that these people have no life at all where they come from." *(emphasize; conclude by saying)*

A priest ______________________

____

____

____

____

4 REPORTED SPEECH: QUESTIONS

›› SB page 134, Grammar checkpoint

Some high school students are asking a visitor from the UN refugee agency about the organization and its work. Report the students' questions for the school magazine. Use the introductory verbs in brackets.

1 "When was the UN refugee agency founded?" *(ask)*

Eli ______________________ the UN refugee agency ______________________ .

2 "What is the main role of the agency?" *(want to know)*

Joshua ______________________ of the agency ______________________ .

3 "Does the head of the agency have to come from a neutral country like Switzerland?" *(wonder)*

Helen ______________________ the head of the agency ______________________

a neutral country like Switzerland.

4 "Is the agency's head office in New York?" *(ask)*

Grant ______________________ in New York.

5 "In how many countries does the agency have an office?" *(want to know)*

Julie ______________________

6 "What is the biggest problem facing the refugee agency?" *(enquire)*

David ______________________

5 REPORTED SPEECH: REQUESTS

›› SB page 134, Grammar checkpoint

A border guard stops a truck that has just crossed the US-Mexican border into California. He thinks the Mexican driver may be carrying illegal immigrants. Report what the guards tells the driver to do. Use the introductory verbs in brackets.

1 "Switch off the engine." *(tell + the driver)*

The guard ______________________ .

2 "Get out of the cab." *(ask + him)*

He ______________________ .

3 "Give me your driver's license and other documents." *(request + the man)*

The guard ______________________

______________________ .

4 "Open the doors at the back of the truck and don't touch anything." *(order + the Mexican)*

He ______________________

______________________ .

5 "Unload some cases and show me what's behind them." *(instruct + the driver)*

He ______________________

______________________ .

6 "Don't put your hands in your pockets. Keep them where I can see them" (tell + the man)

The guard ______________________

but ______________________ .

6 WORDFIELD: MULTICULTURALISM

›› SB page 129, text

Use the clues to solve the puzzle and find the key word.

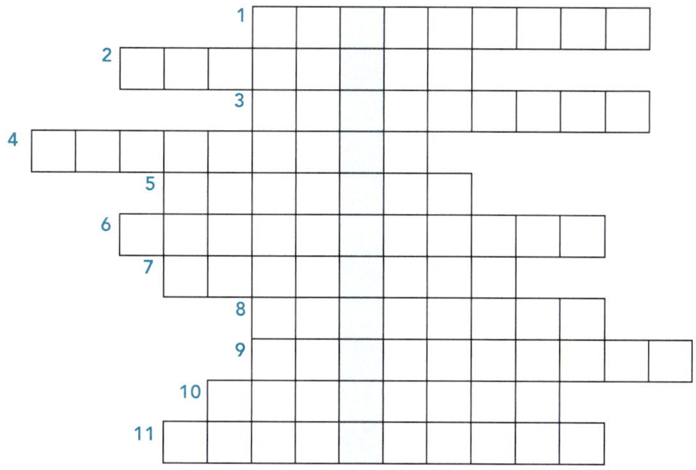

The key word is

_____________________________ .

1 person who goes to another country to live there permanently
2 the way that people think about something is their ... to it
3 Leo Jimenez's original nationality
4 noun form of adjective "ethnic"
5 accepted style of clothing, hair, make up etc, particularly among women
6 person who studies changes in population trends
7 adjective meaning person of Spanish heritage
8 a person's family background going back a long way in time
9 noun meaning "always the same"
10 enormously successful entertainment star like, for example, Jennifer Lopez
11 noun form of adjective "popular"

7 FURTHER OPTIONS

›› SB page 133

Tick (✓) the correct statements about the line graph and bar chart.

Graph 1

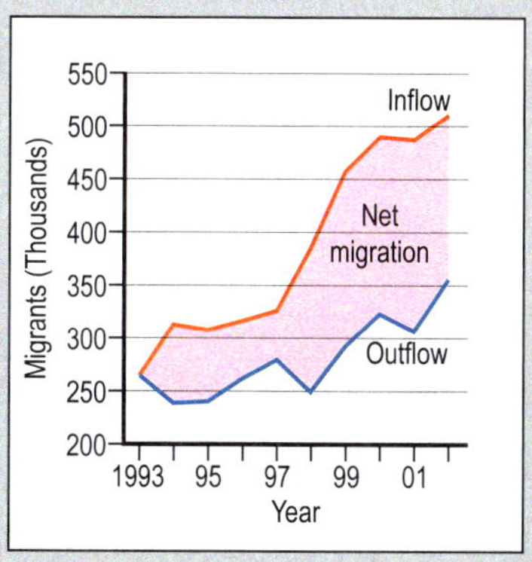

1 During the 10-year period, progressively more people moved away from the UK than moved into it. ☐

2 The lowest outflow was in the year 1994, when around 240,000 people left the UK. ☐

3 During the period as a whole, there was a net inflow of people into the UK. ☐

4 The graph suggests that the UK is not a popular destination among immigrants. ☐

Graph 2

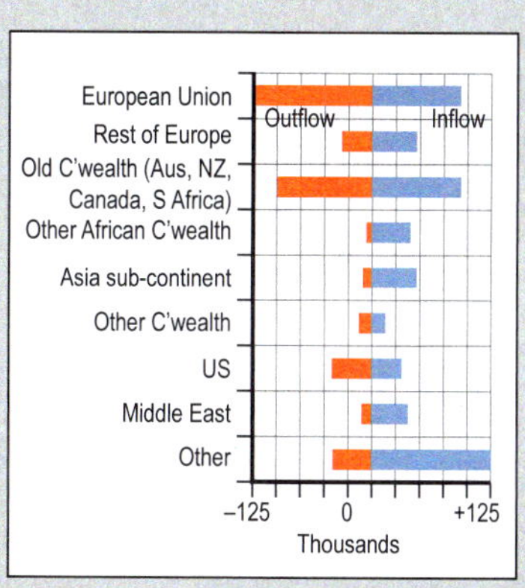

1 Europe supplies more immigrants to the UK than any other region. ☐

2 In 2002, more British people moved to EU countries than the other way round. ☐

3 Many more people come to the UK from "old Commonwealth countries" like Canada and Australia, for example, than leave the UK for those countries. ☐

4 More Americans move to the UK than do British people to the USA. ☐

Source: *National Statistics*

11 Main Course
Crime

1 VOCABULARY

›› SB page 135, Focus

A Fit a crime from the box to the definitions 1–10.

armed robbery | burglary | drunk driving | graffiti-spraying |
manslaughter | mugging | murder | rape | shoplifting | terrorism

1 blowing up, for example, a train to make a political or religious statement ______
2 entering, for example a bank with a gun and demanding money ______
3 causing another person's death without intending to do so ______
4 having sexual intercourse without the other person's consent ______
5 painting designs on buildings without the owner's consent ______
6 removing goods from a store without paying for them ______
7 intentionally taking sb's life after careful planning ______
8 breaking into a building to steal sb's property ______
9 attacking sb in the street to steal their bag, wallet ______
10 being in charge of a vehicle while under the influence of alcohol ______

B How serious are the above crimes? Sort the crimes into a column that gives your own opinion and then use the material to say why.

Very serious	Serious	Not so serious

(to) be / commit a crime against a person
(to) be / commit a crime against property
(to) kill/injure innocent people
(to) behave irresponsibly
(to) cause death/injury
(to) plan a crime
(to) put the safety of others at risk

2 GRAMMAR: ADVERB ORDER

›› SB page 144, Grammar checkpoint

Use arrows to put the adverbs of frequency into the sentences.

1 I'm afraid the police don't patrol the streets. very frequently

2 Liberal commentators claim that poverty causes crime. always

3 Harsh punishment stops people from committing crimes. seldom

4 I enjoy a good crime novel. now and then

5 There is an increase in street crime at Christmas. usually

6 Unfortunately, people leave valuables in their cars. sometimes

7 There's no point in reporting trivial crimes to the police. often

8 You should lock the doors. every night

3 GRAMMAR: WORD ORDER

›› SB page 144, Grammar checkpoint

Spot the mistake: All the sentences have one word order mistake. Use arrows to correct it.

1 The prime minister is opening the new Marsh Prison tomorrow in Leeds.

2 Prime ministers usually do not open prisons, but this is a particularly important occasion.

3 Marsh Prison is different from traditional prisons completely.

4 Marsh Prison is more like a hotel than a fortress unlike traditional prisons.

5 The cells are bigger for example and have a separate toilet and shower like in a hotel.

6 Each cell is just occupied by one prisoner.

7 And prisoners only will spend twelve hours a day in their cells.

8 Prisoners will spend the rest of their time usually doing a useful job or job training.

9 Some conservatives complain of course that prisoners are not on holiday.

10 But supporters say that we must find an answer in traditional prisons to the problem of suicide.

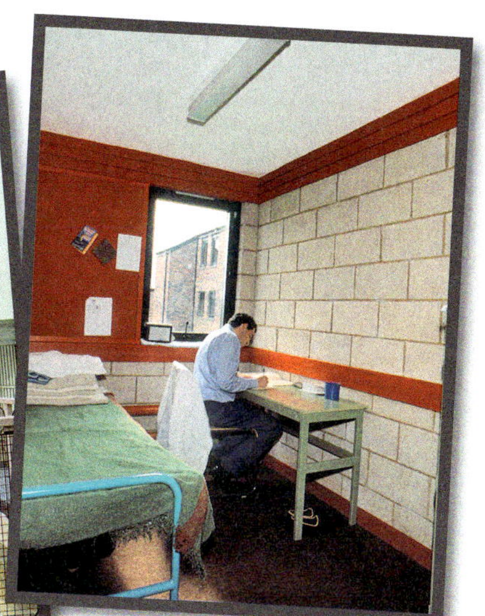

4 BUILDING SKILLS: GIVING A TALK

›› SB page 141, exercise 4

You are giving a talk on the death penalty in the USA. You introduce your talk by referring to the bar chart below about American public opinion on this issue. Read the jumbled sentences 1–8 and use the numbers to link them to the bar chart.

1 At 60 % in favour, the figure for Independents was between these two extremes.

2 Finally, let's look at religion. Here, at 71 % for capital punishment, white protestants were well above the national average, while at 67 % white catholics were not quite so sure.

3 People without any formal religious affiliation voted 59 % in favour.

4 For all that, the biggest differences were found in opinion for or against by political affiliation.

5 However, the survey found big differences by racial, political and religious affiliation (*Zugehörigkeit*).

6 For example, while 78 % of Republicans were in favour of capital punishment, this applied to only 49 % of Democrats.

7 In the survey, 62 % of all respondents were in favour of the death penalty, and 32 % opposed it.

8 Looking at race first, while 68% of whites favoured the death penalty, only 40 % of blacks did so.

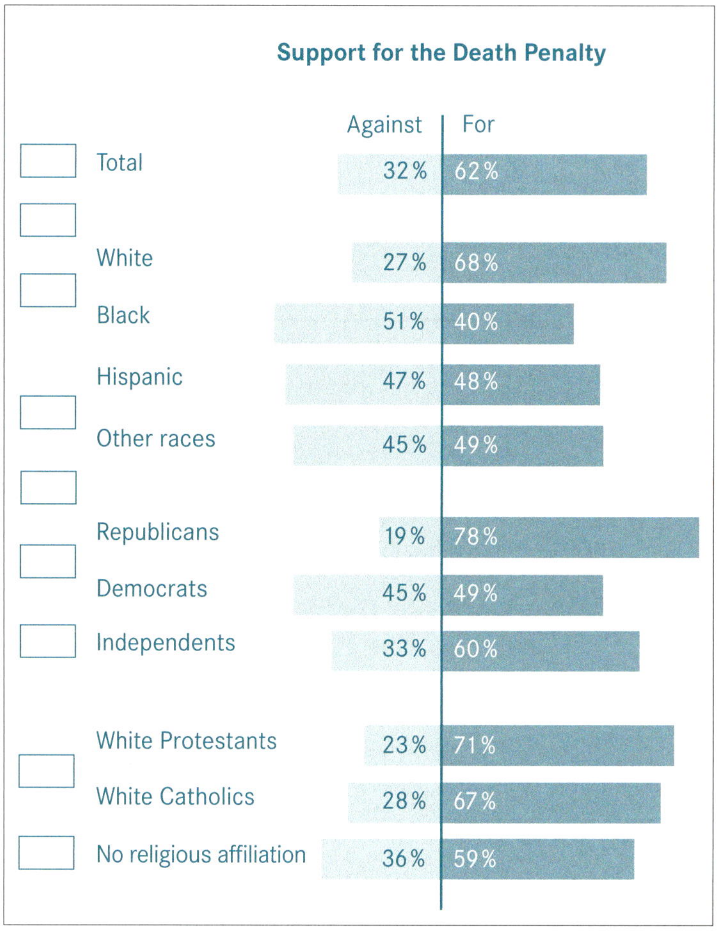

Source: *Pew Research Center 2007*

9 The result for Hispanics was 48 % for and 47 % against, and that for people of other races was 49 % and 45 % respectively.

5 WORDFIELD: CRIME

Find the English equivalents of these German words in the wordsquare on page 59.

1 Abschreckung ______________________

2 bestechlich ______________________

3 Bestechung ______________________

4 gnadenlos ______________________

5 Ladendieb ______________________

6 Mord ______________________

7 New Yorker Polizeibehörde (Abkürzung) ______________________

8 Rassismus ______________________

9 Raubüberfall ______________________

10 Strafmaß ______________________

11 Toleranz ______________________

12 Vergewaltigung ______________________

M	E	R	C	I	L	E	S	S	B	O	L	G	A	V
I	U	T	M	W	E	N	O	O	B	X	F	A	E	S
E	N	R	P	R	O	L	S	E	N	T	E	N	C	E
A	B	V	D	S	H	U	H	A	D	E	S	V	I	S
H	T	H	I	E	N	T	O	L	E	R	A	N	C	E
I	U	F	S	K	R	E	P	E	A	G	S	I	O	T
B	R	I	B	E	R	Y	L	C	E	D	D	Y	R	S
V	O	C	H	E	S	A	I	P	L	U	M	B	R	E
O	B	E	A	T	H	S	F	E	M	O	I	S	U	T
B	B	P	I	L	M	S	T	P	A	R	N	Y	P	D
M	E	F	I	E	G	E	E	A	C	L	O	T	T	R
N	R	I	D	E	T	E	R	R	E	N	T	D	A	T
P	Y	S	C	H	P	R	I	O	F	S	I	D	A	X

You have to look in these directions!

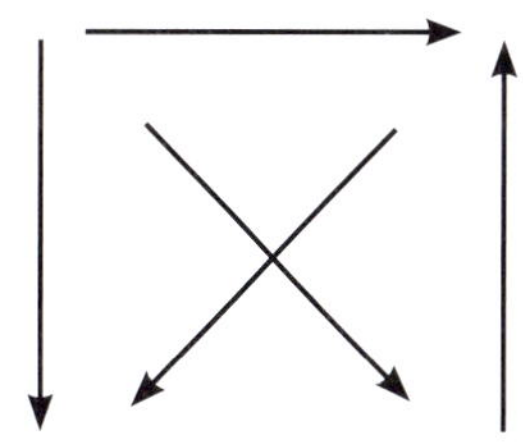

6 FURTHER OPTIONS

›› SB page 143

Study the bar chart about crime in the EU and complete the statements.

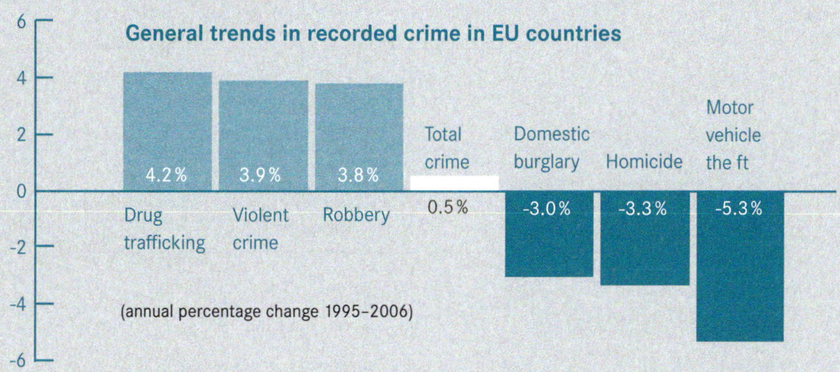

Source: *Eurostat*

1 In the period 1995 to 2006, (total crime / EU / increase / 0.5 %)

____

2 At a plus of 4.2 %, (drug trafficking / show / biggest increase / all / type / crime)

____

3 Also on the growth side, (cases / violent crime / robbery / grow / 3.9 % / 3.8 % / respectively)

____

4 However, the chart also demonstrates (that / type / crime / decrease / sharply)

____

5 For example, (case / domestic burglary / fall / 3.0 %)

____

6 Moreover, the (chart / show / incident / homicide / also / go down / markedly / 3.3 %)

____

7 According to the crime statistics, (at 6.3 % / biggest decrease / be / in / theft / motor vehicles)

____

8 This is surprising, perhaps, (as / a lot / people / western Europe / still / think / theft / expensive car / be / one / commonest crime)

____

12 Main Course
Future life, future living

1 VOCABULARY: DEFINITIONS

›› SB page 146, text

A Link a word/expression from the box with a definition.

announce | astonishing | ban | boycott | calf | current | derive from sth. | ingredient | offspring | onset | prematurely | vast quantity

1 refusal to trade in a product, usually for ethical reasons ____________
2 the young of an animal ____________
3 adjective meaning 'present' in the sense of 'now' ____________
4 make public in speech or writing ____________
5 have its origins in sth. ____________
6 noun meaning 'veto' ____________
7 (here) product that goes into food ____________
8 adjective meaning 'extremely surprising' ____________
9 (here) young of a cow ____________
10 synonym for 'huge amount' ____________
11 adverb meaning 'earlier than expected or planned' ____________
12 noun meaning 'beginning', 'start' ____________

B Complete the sentences with a word from the box.

1 Many countries have introduced a ____________ on smoking in public places.
2 Personal names like 'Baker' and 'Miller' ____________ the names of jobs.
3 We can learn a lot from elephants. They raise their ____________ together.
4 Do you have a ____________ bus timetable, please?
5 Susan's baby was born ____________ but it is going to be fine.
6 It's ____________ that the central banks didn't notice what was happening.

2 VOCABULARY: COLLOCATIONS

›› SB page 146, text

Form collocations by adding a noun from the box to the nouns in the list.
⚠ Collocation: Two nouns, e.g. 'fruit juice', 'fillet steak', that are often used together.

~~animals~~ | calf | farming | fiction | herd | infection | laws | officials | suffering | talks

1 farm *animals*
2 emergency ____________
3 EU ____________
4 health ____________
5 Holstein ____________
6 clone ____________
7 science ____________
8 dairy ____________
9 animal ____________
10 lung ____________

3 MULTIPLE MATCHING: SPEAKERS AND STATEMENTS

›› SB page 149–150, text

Match the speakers A–H to the statements 1–8.

A	Alison Fox, eco-activist	E	Helen Bond, company executive
B	Brian Moore, vegetable grower	F	Ken Oldham, supermarket buyer
C	Dr Harry Sutton, biologist	G	Sarah Clarke, government health official
D	Dr Susan Edwards, family doctor	H	Ted Davis, dairy farmer

1. To ensure the health of our herd, we only allow our best cows to breed. ☐
2. *From my point of view as a grower, the biggest commercial advantage of GM tomatoes is that they do not need so much expensive fertilizer.* ☐
3. *GM farming could be a disaster because nobody can say how GM plants interact with natural ones.* ☐
4. My colleagues and I are very worried that the antibiotic-resistant genes in GM plants could reduce the effectiveness of the antibiotics we use in medicine. ☐
5. **In spite of all the dramatic warnings in the media, in fact there's no evidence that GM food has bad effects.** ☐
6. We sell GM fruit and vegetables mainly because it has a longer shelf life. That makes business sense. ☐
7. I don't know what consumers are so worried about, frankly. GM food is subject to very strict regulation to ensure that it is safe. ☐
8. Universal Biotech Inc. is spending millions of dollars on solving the problem of 'superweeds', and I'm sure we'll succeed. ☐

4 BUILDING SKILLS: TRANSLATING ENGLISH INTO GERMAN

Translate the sentences into German. Take special care with the highlighted parts.

1 Unfortunately, we have made little progress towards controlling cloning.

____

2 Several pieces of valuable furniture were damaged in the fire.

____

3 The news about the cloning of humans is terrifying.

____

4 You will find a lot of information on cloning on the internet, but some of it is nonsense.

____

5 Not all the scientists that are doing cloning experiments are responsible.

____

6 The doctor has told me to eat less and do more exercise in future.

____

7 Bob has been studying biology ever since he was able to read.

____

8 The university stopped the experiments because several scientists were breaking the law.

____

9 It is said that human life will be completely changed by advances in medicine.

____

10 It is feared that even more digitalization could lead to a complete loss of privacy.

____

5 GRAMMAR PROBLEMS

›› SB page 154, Grammar checkpoint

Cross out the incorrect alternative.

1 My ex and I live in the same village. I can't avoid meeting/to meet him sometimes, can I?
2 You'll find two pairs of scissors/scissors in the drawer.
3 Is that the man which/who caused the accident?
4 We're looking forward to come/coming to your party on Saturday.
5 Jack didn't go/hasn't gone on holiday last year because he was ill.
6 I am/have been at this school for two years now.
7 My mum and dad are flying/fly to Florida this afternoon.
8 I am waiting/have been waiting to see the doctor for nearly three hours now.
9 Anna Netrebko sings the role of Violetta wonderfully/wonderfully the role of Violetta.
10 The Bartons live in Station Road in the flats/in the flats in Station Road.
11 We had an ice cream while we waited/were waiting for the movie to start.
12 I am cycling/cycle to school every day.
13 Jane is going to work/will work as a sales assistant in the summer.
14 If you won a lot of money, what will you do/would you do?
15 I'd like six slices ham/slices of ham, please.
16 The traffic jam was caused by sheep/sheeps on the road.
17 The driver would have lived if the ambulance would come/had come more quickly.
18 My brother had to do/must do two years in the army when he was 18.
19 Would you like to try on these shoes or those ones/shoes?
20 My computer was made/was make in China.

6 WORDFIELD: WORD SNAKES

Divide up the letters into words and insert the missing punctuation to make correct sentences.

atendencytogetillnessessuchascanceranddiabetesisprogrammedbyapersonsDNA

foodpoisoningisoftencausedbysomebodyscarelessnessbetweenthefarmgateandthesupermarketshelf

7 FURTHER OPTIONS

›› SB page 153

The Da Vinci Institute in Louisville, Colorado, is a research organization or "think tank" that specializes in predicting the future.

Here are the eight greatest inventions of the next 50 years selected from the Da Vinci Institute's Museum of Future Inventions. They are in no particular order.

Put the eight inventions in your own order of importance.

1 Endless energy from mirrors orbiting the earth and reflecting the sun's energy to power stations below. Consumers will only pay for maintaining the equipment. The energy will be free. ☐

2 A waste converter that uses nanotechnology to convert rubbish into plastic-like materials. his will solve both waste disposal problems and replace plastics that can no longer be manufactured from petroleum, as at present. ☐

3 A means of changing regional weather to suit short-term human needs, for example guaranteeing dry, sunny weather during Wimbledon week. ☐

4 Solving the problem of identity theft with absolutely secure biological ID chips buried under the skin of every human on earth from birth to death. ☐

5 An automatic personalized house run by robots controlled by computers. ☐

6 A genetic cure for all forms of cancer as well as conditions like diabetes and dementia in old age. Such medical technologies will be necessary as the length of human life increases to 110 years or more. ☐

7 Repacing or regenerating human sense organs – sight, hearing, touch, taste – by means of computer chips. ☐

8 An 'instant sleep chamber' enabling users to enjoy eight hours deep sleep in as many seconds. his would increase the length of conscious human life by about one third. ☐

Focus on Success – The new edition: Allgemeine Ausgabe Workbook
wurde geplant und entwickelt von der Redaktion Moderne Fremdsprachen
des Cornelsen Verlags, Berlin.

Verfasser: David Clarke, Witten
Michael Macfarlane, Oxford

Projektleitung: Jim Austin
Verlagsredaktion: Andreas Goebel
Außenredaktion: James Abram
Bildredaktion: Gertha Maly
Layout und technische Umsetzung: sign, Berlin
Umschlaggestaltung: werkstatt für gebrauchsgrafik, Berlin

Illustrationen: Oxford Designers & Illustrators
Bildquellen: Cover: Fotofinder: A1PIX; DLR; istockphoto; Fotofinder: Karlheinz Oster (RF Fotos) Alamy: S. 7/O. Dimier, S. 14/1/Alvery&Towers Picture Library, S. 14/4, S. 14/7/Somos Group, S. 24/Image Source Pink, S. 25/Dynamic Graphics, S. 38/Comstock, S. 44, S. 49/B2M Productions, S. 57/1/2/ Aardvark; Shutterstock: S. 10, S. 14/2, S. 14/3, S. 14/5, S. 36 (RM Fotos) Alamy: S. 12/J. Wiedel, S. 21/S. Kiefer, S. 50/T. Koene, S. 52/J. Morgan, S. 56/H. Barlow; Cinetext: S. 27; Fotofinder: S. 11/ Bildagentur-online, S. 16/photoplexus, S. 20/Visum/J. Rezac, S. 46/ImageSource; Gettyimages: S. 14/6/P. Adams, S. 14/8/AltrendoImages
Cartoons: S. 31/CartoonStock
Textquellen: S. 51 'Conversation Piece' from *Collected Poems*, Macmillan's Children's Books. © Gareth Owen 2000, by permission of Rogers, Coleridge & White Ltd on behalf of the author.

www.cornelsen.de

1. Auflage, 2. Druck 2010

Alle Drucke dieser Auflage sind inhaltlich unverändert und können im Unterricht nebeneinander verwendet werden.

Druck: Himmer AG, Augsburg

ISBN: 978-3-06-020230-0

Inhalt gedruckt auf säurefreiem Papier aus nachhaltiger Forstwirtschaft.